To *from* *Kent*

GUIDELINES FOR CONTEMPORARY CATHOLICS

Scripture Today

John L. Boyle, S.J.

THE THOMAS MORE PRESS

Chicago, Illinois

ISBN 0-88347-242-2

TABLE OF CONTENTS

For my Mother

I. INTRODUCTION

SIGNS of interest in Scripture today appear from the popularity of TV evangelists to newspaper articles on the latest finds in archaeology or modern theories on biblical interpretation. Even as we watch on television a golfer trying to get out of a sand trap, a placard in the background reminds us (Jn 3:16) "God so loved the world. . . ." Both fundamentalist groups on the right and liberation theologians on the left point to the Bible to prove the rightness of their cause.

A past cover picture on *Time* magazine was a modern mosaic of Jesus, with parts of the picture coming from icons of the past to modern photographs. The cover article was occasioned by the movie *The Last Temptation of Christ,* but the article was essentially a compilation of various approaches to the history and person of Jesus. It was not a babel of voices, but it did represent various tendencies in contemporary research on the New Testament.

This small book will attempt to present some background to the contemporary approaches to Scripture. The first chapter will point out the importance of Scripture in the early Church, interpreted in the light of Christ; and how both Scripture (the Old Testament) and the traditions about Jesus were incorporated into the form and reality called "Gospel." The next chapter will be on the development and closure of the canon of Scripture; then a chapter on the interpretation of Scripture during the period of the Fathers and Middle Ages. There follows a brief overview of scholarship from the time of the rise of historical consciousness, with the Catholic reaction down to Vatican II. The final chapter will give some examples of a more recent literary approach to Scripture.

This brief overview covering two millennia is bound to be somewhat simplistic; but, hopefully, it will show, in some way, how we got to where we are today.

II. SCRIPTURE IN THE NEW TESTAMENT

1) "According to the Scriptures"

"SCRIPTURE today isn't what it used to be." Some in the synagogue, listening to the followers of Jesus explaining Scripture, could easily make this observation. These Nazareans, followers of "the Way," claimed that the hope and expectations of the people of Israel, voiced in the prophets, the Psalms, and in the Law itself, had reached their fulfillment in Jesus, in his death and resurrection. God had vindicated not only Jesus, but had fulfilled his design in history and his promise to the people. The apparent defeat of Jesus and what he stood for was actually the expected "Day of the Lord," the victory over death, and the beginning of the transformation of Israel.

They claimed that this event was the source of the promised outpouring of the Spirit which the prophets foretold, the new covenant between God and the people. And the audience should have some experience of this in the preaching and living witness of these followers of Jesus.

11

John L. Boyle, S. J.

In this preaching, various key texts were presented to show their fulfillment in Jesus, the Christ. But there was no question of logical proof. The challenge was presented that in this event and in this person everything came together. God's promise to David, and before that to Abraham, had been kept, but in a surprising way. The expectations of the people had been answered in an unexpected way. Various themes which were apparently separate in tradition, such as the Suffering Servant and the Glorious King, converged in the event and person of Jesus.

And the preachers believed that they were speaking for God as did the prophets of old. They were calling for a change of heart and acceptance through faith of the gift offered through their message. As the prophets had spoken "the word of the Lord," so God was present in the preaching of the Christians.

As they pointed out the convergence of texts and themes in the event of Jesus, so they called attention to the "fit" in the message preached, the witness of those who preached, and the nature of the acceptance in faith. In his letter to the church at Corinth, Paul reminds them of the message of the scandal of the Cross: God's power was presented not in a powerful way but in weakness. And those who accepted it were not the learned or the powerful, but the weak. Message, manner, and response of faith all converge. (Cf. I Cor 1:17-2:5.)

From this paradox of a victory over death through a humiliating death, the pattern of paradox throughout Scripture also found its center. The last are first, the rejected are accepted, God raises up the poor. And hopes based on seemingly contrary promises also converged. A human Messiah was promised to lead the people, but the Lord said that he would rule the people. A new Temple was promised, but God's dwelling is not in a house of stone.

The prophets said that the Gentiles would share in the blessings of a restored Israel by coming to its center in Jerusalem. But, to the surprise of the Christian community, this was taking place through the Church—the true renewed Israel—being driven out of Jerusalem to other lands and nations. The Jewish nation whose identity was grounded in Scripture would surely accept this message which fulfilled Scripture; yet, it was the outsider, the Gentile, who seemed to be more open. The fulfillment of the promise and expectation continued to appear in a totally unexpected way. It was always a surprise.

The openness of the Gentiles was a surprise. This experience led to a deeper reflection on the place of the Gentiles in God's promise to Israel. It also led to a deeper awareness of the mission of Jesus who was sent "only to the lost sheep of the House of Israel."

In Matthew's Gospel, this acceptance of the pagans is already foreshadowed in the worship of the Magi. But in the missionary instruction to the twelve (Matt 10), they, too, are sent only to the lost sheep of the House of Israel. They are to go "nowhere among the Gentiles and enter no town of the Samaritans" (Matt 10:5). Curiously, however, in Matthew they go nowhere at all. In Mark and in Luke, the twelve are sent as missionaries during the earthly ministry of Jesus. But not in Matthew. Their true mission only begins when the risen Lord sends them to all the nations. This means that the words "lost sheep of the House of Israel" have been given a wider extension of meaning. But it took the Church, the true Israel, a while to fully recognize this.

This growing recognition explains the emphasis on the acceptance of the Gentiles in the traditions about Jesus in the Gospels, e.g., the cures of the Syro-Phoenician woman's daughter and the centurion's servant. And in Luke's Gospel, after Jesus gives his opening sermon in his native town (Luke 4:16-30), he is rejected by his own who even try to kill him precisely because he claimed that the grace of God's year of favor is destined for the outsiders, the Gentiles.

2) Christ, the Key

In I Cor 15, Paul points out how the Christ-event is the fulfillment of Scriptures: "Christ died for our sins according to the Scriptures. . . . and was raised on the third day according to the Scriptures." His followers look forward to seeing Christ. But Paul also points out how we should look back and read or reread Scripture in the light of Christ. In II Cor 3:7-18, Paul says that without Christ, Scripture is a

Scripture Today

dead letter and leads to death; with Christ as the key to interpretation, Scripture is alive and leads to a growing assimilation of Christ at the center of our living. Using the example of the veil over the face of Moses at the revelation of the Law, Paul says that the Jews who have refused the revelation of Christ still have a veil over their face in understanding the true meaning of the common religious texts which both Jew and Christian read. Through Christ the veil is removed. With Christ as the focus, Scriptures come alive. "When one turns to the Lord, the veil is removed. Now the Lord is the Spirit, and where the Spirit of the Lord is, there is freedom. And we all, with unveiled face, beholding the glory of the Lord, are being changed into his likeness from one degree of glory to another; for this comes from the Lord who is the Spirit."

The Lord is the Spirit in two corresponding ways: as the key to understanding Scripture and as the living spiritual presence who opens the eyes and heart to understand. That is why Paul says that Christians are led not simply to a deeper understanding of a text but are gradually being changed into his likeness. Luke expresses the same thing in the appearance of the risen Christ to the two on the way to Emmaus (Luke 24:27). "Beginning with Moses and all the prophets, he interpreted in all the Scriptures the things concerning himself." After they finally recognized him in the breaking of the bread, they said, "Did not our hearts burn within us while he spoke to us on the way, while he opened to us the Scriptures?" (Luke 24:32).

John L. Boyle, S. J.

3) The Gospel

The term for Christian preaching quickly came to be "the Gospel" (*euaggelion*). The general background for the use of this word was the role of the messenger who announced to the people a decisive victory (or defeat) and/or the name of the ruler who assumed authority at this proclamation. In an age before newspapers or instant communication, the role of this messenger was obviously important. More than a town-crier, the herald carried the authority of the ruler. With the official proclamation, the result of the event or the authority of the ruler took place.

In was only natural, then, that this social reality and image be taken up into Scripture. Isaiah looked forward to the herald who would announce the "good news" (gospel) to the people. The event is the end of exile, a new Exodus, a rebirth of the people, a return from death to life. And the ruler: "the Lord rules" (Isa 52:7).

The Christian preachers, reading Scripture in the light of the Christ-event, realized that the event Isaiah looked forward to was in its truest sense the victory over sin and death in the death and resurrection of Jesus. And the ruler? "Jesus is Lord." A more important difference was that the proclamation of the event and naming of the ruler by the Christian herald did not take place automatically. It called for a change of heart and free acceptance: acknowledging the meaning of this event as God's fulfillment of a promise

16

Scripture Today

and a call to personal attachment in faith to Jesus as Lord. Another word for this Christian proclamation which derives from the name of this herald of the event (*keryx*) was "the proclamation" (*kerygma*).

If not the first to use the word "gospel" for his preaching, Paul used it the most. The Gospel of the Cross was not simply the victory over death, but the end of the radical separation of the people from God through their sin and infidelity. It was the Day of Expiation: Atonement. And, as Paul saw more and more clearly, it was this Event which decisively broke down the wall of separation between Jew and Gentile. And it was for this message, as central to the Gospel, that Paul claimed he was set apart and called to preach.

What was central to this Gospel, in Paul and in others, was the radically new life which this Event inaugurated for the Christian: sharing the same Spirit by which Jesus was raised from the dead, the Christians were called to a new life in mutual hope and love.

For Paul the whole Gospel was simply Jesus, the Christ. Beyond that, the content was not fixed but flexible. It was not like a defined Creed. In addition to a message accepted in faith, it could include different ethical or moral instructions to the various needs of the different churches. Sometimes the word Gospel referred to the act of proclamation or the work of the missionary. Sometimes it referred to the content of the message itself. And often it meant the response of faith. Paul talks of it as "the obedience": the

17

obedient response of faith of the community which has at its center the very obedience of Christ. All of these are aspects of one reality; they all converge.

This living reality was also communicated by the influence of a shared faith. Paul and the others were "models." The community itself was a Gospel spreading to others the "aroma" of Christ. Paul did not hesitate to encourage the churches to imitate him, not simply his words. They were to imitate the other churches, even to imitate God. The Gospel was a shared life in union with the living Christ. Christ was the message, Christ the messenger, Christ the center of a shared life.

Based on a past reality, the Event of the Cross, the Gospel was directed to a present life. It was not a recounting of the mortal or earthly ministry of Jesus. Paul was, surprisingly for us, not much interested in that. "If I knew Jesus according to the flesh, I know him that way no longer" (II Cor 5:16). For Paul the "life of Christ" was not a past reality. "I live, no longer I, Christ lives in me" (Gal 2:20). The fact that Paul, unlike the other Apostles, did not experience the earthly career of Jesus, is not the main reason for this emphasis. For him the new order or new creation was what is decisive: "the old has passed away" (II Cor 5:17).

Christians should look out for the needs of others more than their own not because of a teaching of Jesus but based on the meaning of the Event which they celebrated in a hymn. "Have this mind which was in Christ" (in the obedience of his death) (Cf. Phil 2:5). And Paul's recalling of the

Last Supper to the Corinthians was not to point out what happened then but the meaning of the present experience of their worship and the meaning of the Eucharist in their lives (I Cor 11:23-26).

Though Paul's Gospel had a distinctive quality, he insists that it was in continuity with the common tradition: "I hand on to you what was handed on to me" (I Cor 15:3). And it was in continuity with the promise of God expressed, in various ways, in Scripture. But, surprising as it may be, he doesn't say, except rarely, that it was in continuity with the teachings and actions of Jesus back in his earthly ministry. It was up to the later "Gospels" to bring this out.

4) The Gospel in the Gospels

Collections of the sayings of Jesus were, of course, important and authoritative. But what is more important than the fact that Jesus said them to a certain audience at a certain place back then was that Jesus is present to the community now. And the memory of the deeds of Jesus and his teaching back then was to flesh out and deepen the commitment and union of Christians with him now.

The fact that the earthly career of Jesus was not part of the Gospel, in Paul's approach, might have led to two separate traditions: the Gospel emphasizing the present, and the memoirs of the Apostles emphasizing the past. But very early these memories of the earthly career of Jesus, reflected on in the Church, were incorporated into the reality of the Gospel.

The Gospel of Mark is the only one to refer to itself as a "Gospel." We are tempted to say that this writing is obviously a Gospel because it recounts what Jesus did and said back then. But from the meaning of the word "Gospel," which emphasizes a present reality, this work of Mark is apparently not a Gospel but a kind of biography of the earthly Jesus. It is important to recognize that Mark and the other three Gospels are not different biographies of Jesus. It is important to read them as Gospels.

(a) Some Examples

One example that shows how the Jesus tradition has been drawn into the genre of Gospel is the beginning of Mark: "The gospel of Jesus Christ, the Son of God." Clearly Jesus is the theme and object of the Gospel message and precisely as Christ and Son of God. After the scriptural citation which shows that the Gospel is "according to the Scriptures," we have the ministry of the Baptist calling the people to repentance; the voice from heaven, at the Baptism of Jesus, calling him the beloved Son; a brief and mysterious account of Jesus' trial in the desert; and then the preaching of Jesus.

We are given the tradition that Jesus preached of God's reign or Kingdom; but then Mark says that Jesus said: "Repent and believe in the Gospel." A word which had referred

Scripture Today

to Jesus as the object of the message now has the historical Jesus as the source of the preaching. In a way, this had already been implied in the early Christian message. Object of the preaching, Jesus was present as risen Lord calling, through the Christian heralds, to repentance and union with him in faith. What Mark does is to push back the beginning of the Gospel to the first preaching of Jesus. He thus incorporates the past traditions about Jesus into the present reality of "Gospel."

An important theme in all four Gospels is the call of the first disciples. The account in Matthew and Mark is essentially the same; but in Luke and in John it is quite different. In Matthew and Mark, the disciples are in boats beside the sea. Jesus comes by and abruptly calls them. Though they had never met him before, they leave their former occupation at once. Jesus says that they will be fishermen in another sense: they will gather people together. The key points in the account are the location of the sea, the suddenness of the call and the immediacy of response, and the leaving behind of possessions and family.

The scene is not described as an account of what exactly happened back then but as a paradigm of discipleship now: what it means for a Christian to be called to discipleship. Later on in these two Gospels, Jesus says every one of his followers must be prepared to leave behind possessions and family.

In Luke's account of the first call, Peter already knows Jesus; he had cured his mother-in-law. After the miraculous catch of fish (Luke 5), Peter proclaims himself a sinner (a privileged group in Luke's Gospel), and Jesus proclaims in the presence of the others that from this moment on he will be catching not fish but people, drawing them in alive. Luke ends the account by saying that "they left everything." He says this of the first disciples because it is true of any disciple: "he must leave everything" (Luke 14:33). The call of the first disciples is presented as a paradigm of discipleship for all.

John's account seems, at first sight, to say little of discipleship. The first disciples were followers of the Baptist. Indeed, it is implied that Jesus himself had been a follower "who came after" John: an expression of discipleship. "They asked where he was staying and they stayed with him" (John 1:38-39). It seems like an ordinary encounter. But when we translate the expression literally ("They asked where he remains and they remained with him"), this expresses the basis of discipleship in the Gospel of John. In the parable of the vine, at the center of the last discourse, remaining with Jesus (or, rather, in him) is said to be the only source of a fruitful life.

In the four Gospels, then, the account of the call of the first disciples expresses what it means to be a disciple now in the present life of the Church. It is important to enter into the story with one's imagination. But if you attempt to get behind the story to what actually happened back then you can miss the point of what the Gospels are about. John's account is quite different from the others. In Luke, Peter is already a friend of Jesus though not yet a disciple. It is useless to try to discover the precise event behind the Gospels because the writers are not interested in that. They are trying to express something which is far more important.

(b) Some Translations

Some expressions in the New American Bible have been translated differently in its more recent translation of the New Testament prepared for the liturgy. Sometimes the older translation betrayed an attempt to express what happened back then more than what was being presented in the Gospel.

Three examples:

In the first translation of the call of the disciples, they are seen at a lake. The reason is clear: the Lake of Genessareth is a lake; it is not a sea. The writers of Matthew and Mark knew that, but they use the word sea because of what the word "sea" connotes in Scripture: the realm of chaos from which the Master of the Sea rescues the people. In the scene of "the storm at sea," the early Church did not recollect a squall on a lake back then but a present stormy experience of crossing over to the other side, the land of the Gentiles. Jesus chiding the disciples for their lack of faith is heard as the voice of Jesus to a troubled community, encouraging her to hope, to rely on the presence of Christ in her midst.

A second change for the better in translation is the story of Jairus and his sick daughter. He addresses Jesus as

John L. Boyle, S. J.

"Sir," a title of respect. The term *Kyrios* could be a title of respect back then, but in the Gospel tradition *Kyrios* means Lord. It is true that someone back then could have meant the term *Kyrios* as a polite expression. It is also true that he didn't speak Greek. But the question is: What does it mean in Matthew's Gospel? The newer translation of "Lord" is a change for the better.

A third example of an improved translation is the account of the cure of Bartimaeus before the entrance of Jesus into Jerusalem (Mark 10:46-52). After the cure, the NAB translates: "he followed him up the road." Presumably, he accompanied Jesus up to Jerusalem and then bade him a fond farewell. Once again the translator tries to describe the scene as an event back then.

But the word *hodos,* which is translated here as road, is used seven times in this section of Mark's Gospel to mean the "way" of Jesus: the mystery of his death and resurrection which the disciples are called to enter into and share. This is the "way" to enter into the Reign of God. Happily, the translation has now been changed to "he followed him on the way." After all, the importance of this word and theme appears at the outset of Mark's Gospel when he fuses a text from Malachi with that of Isaiah: "I will send my messenger before your face who shall prepare your way; the voice of one crying in the wilderness: 'prepare the way of the Lord'." The word road here would surely miss the point.

Scripture Today

A last example will be noted of what would be a better translation, but which was not made. In all four Gospels, Jesus on the Cross is given something to drink. Most translators say "cheap wine" or "common wine." But the word is vinegar. Since it is unlikely that straight vinegar was offered to Jesus back then, one explanation is that they gave him the cheap wine which the Roman soldiers drank. A better guess is that they offered him water to which vinegar was added; it is better for quenching thirst. But the word in all four Gospels is vinegar. And the reader/listener of the Gospels knew what kind of vinegar: Ps 69 brand vinegar. "In my thirst they gave me vinegar to drink" (Ps 69:21). This allusion to Ps 69 in the Passion account, along with other citations of Scripture, underlines the belief that somehow God's will, expressed in Scripture, was being fulfilled in an event which most people would see as the absence of God and the ultimate and shameful defeat of Jesus.

Once again, the desire to get behind the text to describe what might have happened back then is to miss the point of the Gospels.

5) Back to Scripture

In the early preaching, certain key texts in Scripture were cited to show that the event of Christ was the fulfillment of God's promises to Israel. But gradually this was seen as the fulfillment of the whole of Scripture read in a more global, inclusive, and unified way. One characteristic of the New Testament which shows this tendency and development is the combining of different texts from the Old Testament to form a new unity.

(a) Combining Texts

Paul feels free to join together a number of texts which in their original contexts had little or nothing to do with one another. For example, in Rom 9 Paul cites a number of texts from Genesis and Exodus to the Prophets with a remarkable freedom. We might call it arbitrary. In 9:25-26, he cites Hos 2:23: "Those who were not my people I will call my people and her who was not my beloved I will call my beloved. And in the very place where it was said 'You are not my people,' they will be called 'sons of the living God'." This is presented as one text even though the first half is a free allusion to Hos 2:23 and the second a citation of Hos 1:10.

In I Cor 15:54b-55, Paul cites Scripture: "Death is swallowed up in victory. O death, where is your victory? O death, where is your sting?" The first half is from Isaiah referring to the future victory over death (Isa 25:8); the second part is from Hoseah in which the Lord calls upon death to punish Israel (Hos 13:14). Paul's free citation not only combines texts from two different prophets, the texts refer to opposing reactions of the Lord: the first a promise, the second a threat. And, joined together, Paul calls it one word of Scripture. This would seem to us an arbitrary reading of Scripture.

This combining of texts to make a point was also used in Jewish interpretation of Scripture; Paul is not unique in this. But the focus of this combining of texts for Paul is always the event of Christ.

Two examples of combining texts can be taken from the Gospels. The beginning of Mark's Gospel is a citation from Isaiah: "Behold, I send my messenger before your face who shall prepare your way; the voice of one crying in the wilderness: 'Prepare the way of the Lord, make his paths straight'." One looks through Isaiah in vain to find the first half of the citation because it is from the prophet Malachi (Mal 3:1). But it is cited as one text from Isaiah. And the original text says: "Behold, I send my messenger before my face who will prepare my way" not "your face" and "your way." In Mark, as in the other Synoptic Gospels, God is not referring to Himself but to another. This is a Christian reading of Scripture in which God is shown to be speaking about Jesus. And in the second half of the citation, the verse (in the Greek translation used in the early Church): "Prepare the way of the Lord, make straight the paths of our God" has been changed to: "make straight the paths of him," namely, the Lord: Jesus. The point of union of the two texts is the expression: "the way of the Lord," which is a principle theme in Mark's Gospel. Once again we find a remarkable freedom in re-reading Scripture in the light of Christ.

Matthew's Passion account refers to the field of blood

bought with the money paid to Judas for his betrayal. Matthew (Matt 27:9-10) cites Jeremiah: "And they took the thirty pieces of silver, the price of him on whom a price had been set by some of the sons of Israel, and they gave them for the potter's field, as the Lord directed me." But the first part is from Zechariah (Zech 11:12-13) referring to the people's rejection of the Lord; the second part is from Jeremiah referring to the field of redemption: the Lord's promise of restoration. And the basis of this restoration is the blood of Christ. The rejection of the people is, remarkably, the occasion for the fulfillment of God's promise of restoration and redemption.

We might call this free combining of texts arbitrary and improper. They would consider it quite natural and to the point. Christ is the key for understanding the whole of Scripture. The different themes and texts of Scripture find their unity in the Christ-event. This combination of texts will continue in the approach of the Fathers.

(b) Type and Allegory

In confronting the problems of the Church at Corinth, Paul warns against self-satisfaction by citing the experience of the Church in the desert (I Cor 10). They, too, ate a spiritual food (bread from heaven) and drank a spiritual drink (water from the rock), "and the rock was Christ" (I Cor 10:4). "Now these things happened to them as types, but they were written down for our instruction upon whom the fulfillment of the ages has come. Therefore, let anyone who thinks he stands, take heed lest he fall" (I Cor 10:11-12).

Paul is reading the desert experience of Israel in the light of Christ. God's active presence with the people then was leading to the definitive presence in Christ. And this event, with its presentation in Scripture, was intended also and especially for the Church. This shows a wider extension of seeing Christ as the fulfillment of Scripture—not simply in prophetic hopes for the future but in narratives of the past.

This typology: events, people, or institutions looking forward to a fulfillment in Christ and the Church is most prominent in the Letter to the Hebrews. Psalm 110 is widely quoted in the New Testament as a Messianic fulfillment text. Hebrews picks up the mention of Melchisedech in the psalm and says that he was a type of Christ. Indeed, the whole institution of worship in the desert (and in the land) was a sketch or shadow of the true worship to come.

Hebrews also quotes Ps 95 which recalls Israel's tempting God in the desert and their being prevented from entering into "my rest." The "rest" of the promised land is interpreted by Hebrews as the sabbath rest of God. The future goal of the people is, then, to enter not the "rest" of the land but the "rest" of God. The Letter to the Hebrews quotes the verse: "Today, when you hear his voice, do not harden your hearts." This reminds the readers/listeners to be open and attentive to the word of the Lord in the present. Indeed, that was the point of the psalm to begin with.

John L. Boyle, S. J.

In the fourth chapter of the Letter to the Galatians, Paul sees the new covenant foreshadowed in the story of Hagar and Sarah (Gen 16). "It is written that Abraham had two sons, one by a slave and one by a free woman. But the son of the slave was born according to the flesh, the son of the free woman through a promise. Now this is an allegory" (Gal 4:22-24). Paul goes on to say that the two women represent the two covenants represented by Mount Sinai and Jerusalem from above, our Mother according to the promised Spirit. In the Scripture, Sinai already prepared for the Sion or Jerusalem of the future which would bring forth many children (Isa 66). Paul picks up this theme and interprets the narrative of the two wives of Abraham in terms of the experienced reality of the Church. He calls this rereading of Scripture in terms of Christ an allegorical reading. This kind of reading will continue during the era of the Fathers.

(c) Back to the Gospels

The Gospel of Paul and the other Gospels all cite Scripture freely, and they allude to this tradition in various ways. But there are different emphases, especially in Matthew and in John. At the beginning of Matthew we find various incidents in the early life of Jesus for which Matthew explicitly cites a part of Scripture fulfilled: the birth of Jesus according to the Spirit, the killing of the innocent children, the return from Egypt, the sojourn in Nazareth, and the place of ministry: Galilee of the nations. The fulfillment texts

Scripture Today

show Jesus as the consummation of the history of Israel and recall earlier events in that history. The events of the history of Israel foreshadow the Event of Christ. This same current will continue throughout the Gospel of Matthew.

The Gospel of John also refers to events in Scripture which foreshadow the Christ-event (the Incarnation), but this Gospel emphasizes more the unity of God's plan. Key figures of Scripture were already attuned to God's design. "Abraham rejoiced to see my day; he saw it and was glad" (John 8:56). "Isaiah saw his glory" (John 12:41). But a more important characteristic of this Gospel is the perspective on the earthly ministry of Jesus as foreshadowing the ministry of the risen Lord in the Church. The various things that Jesus did back then are "signs" of what he would do when the hour had come.

Jesus says to Nicodemus that true belief and real re-birth would only come when he was "lifted up." The Samaritan woman was promised the gift of living water. But this would become an inner source of life only in the future. Jesus gives the bread in the wilderness and declares that he is the true bread. But this bread of life which is his own life shared with the Father can only be shared with his own after he gives his life for the world. The "anointing" of the blind man and the mysterious washing in the pool called Sent foreshadows Christian baptism.

The Gospel of John sees these incidents in the life of the "historical" Jesus in much the same way as Matthew sees the events in the history of Israel: they are signs which foreshadow the true reality which breaks through only with the "glorification" of Jesus, the full revelation of the mystery of God's love.

Through the centuries, these different emphases will be combined in various patterns in the way the Church would read the Scripture.

III. THE CANON OF SCRIPTURE

ALMOST all of the writings which make up the New Testament were read in the churches before the end of the first century. But they were not accepted as a closed collection, considered as Scripture, by the larger Church until the end of the fourth century. Even then, the Apocalypse of John was suspect here and there; and the Letter to the Hebrews was somewhat in doubt in the West. What took the Church so long? A brief survey of the context for the reading of Scripture, the history, and certain problems of the time might help to explain this.

1) The Development

Scripture for the early Church is what we call the Old Testament. It was read in Hebrew and in a free Aramaic translation in the synagogues and in the early Christian gatherings (*ecclesiai*). Each word (synagogue and ecclesia) is a Greek translation of the assembly of the people of Israel.

John L. Boyle, S. J.

The word "church" (ecclesia) became the accepted term for the Christian assembly because it was the preferred term in the Greek Scripture for the gathering of Israel in prayer; but it also had a broader meaning in the Roman world. It also served to show the difference between the Christian community and the synagogue.

From the first proclamation in the synagogue calling for conversion and acceptance of the Christ-event "according to the Scriptures" and acceptance in faith of Jesus as present Lord, the context for the reading of Scripture became the believing Christian community, the church (*ecclesia*) gathered together in prayer and to hear the word of the Lord. Few people read Scripture; they listened to it. And more and more of Scripture, not simply the prophetic oracles, was understood and interpreted in the light of Christ. Paul's Letters give evidence of this deepening and wider understanding of Scripture.

Because of the importance of the extraordinary Apostle Paul, his letters were read along with Scripture not simply to the individual churches to which he sent them but to other churches as well; and they were gathered together into a collection. Since these were read along with Scripture, they began to have an authority along with Scripture.

More important were the sayings of Jesus. Since Scripture was the "word of the Lord," the word of the Lord (Jesus) must be on a par with Scripture. The collection of sayings of Jesus had a great importance because these sayings were

heard not simply as Jesus' words back then, but as express-
ing Jesus' presence to the community now.

The role of the Apostles as eye-witnesses to this historical
period which ushered in the present age, "the last days,"
was also important, and these memoirs or living memory
became part of the "memory" of the churches. These memories of the deeds and words of Jesus were given a context in
the various situations of the churches. The sequence of
events of the Passion naturally took on a distinctive chronological form. But the events before that were given a context
that addressed the needs of the churches. The call to enter
more deeply into the mystery of Christ appeared in the context of Jesus' predictions of his death and resurrection. A
sermon by Jesus, whether long or short, on a mountain or
on a plain, served to bring out the particular emphases of
the individual Gospels. This formation of the Gospels was
finished before the end of the century. But their universal
acceptance as Scripture by the greater Church was something else again.

2) The Closing of the Canon

Together with the writings mentioned, there were others:
some edifying, some silly, some dangerous. Which ones
were to be accepted? The first attempt at a closed canon
of Scripture was by a man named Marcion who thought he

faithfully represented the teaching of Paul. Scripture, or the Law, prepared for the coming of Christ but now is to be discarded; it has served its purpose. "The Letter, Scripture, kills; the Spirit gives life" (II Cor 3:6). The God of love has been revealed; the God of anger of the old dispensation is to be rejected. In his simplified canon, Marcion admitted the Letters of Paul and a shortened version of Luke (omitting Scriptural quotations as having been added by Judaizers). He also had to drop some favorable allusions to Scripture in the Letters of Paul.

This might seem to us not only dangerous but strange. However, on reflection, this view of the Old Testament is still with us today. And so, along with the process of defining the new was the need to affirm and uphold the old.

The view of Marcion in an expanded version was Gnosticism—perhaps the greatest threat to the early Church. Not only was the old to be discarded, but all of history holds humanity in bondage. Material creation comes from an evil "god" or demiurge. We are called to escape from matter and history to an authentic spiritual reality, our true home. The stories of Jesus are symbols of a higher spiritual reality. Since the scenes in the Gospel of John, "the Spiritual Gospel," are presented in a more symbolic way, the Gnostics chose this Gospel as their favorite. Which naturally led many in the churches to consider the Fourth Gospel as dangerous and suspect because it was used by the Gnostics.

Some were hesitant to accept one or another of the Gospels because they were used in a heretical way. Luke was used by Marcion, John by the Gnostics. Some liked Matthew because he seemed to have an "adoptionist" approach (Jesus was adopted as son of God). A few liked Mark because they thought he had a "docetic" approach (Jesus only seemed to be human).

Against the Gnostics and in defense of our present Gospels, Irenaeus (c. 130-200) held strongly to the four-fold Gospel—no more, no less. He points out the symbolism of the four directions, among other uses of the number four. But the main argument was that these Gospels and no others go back to the Apostles. Luke was a disciple of Paul, and Mark of Peter. There was only one Gospel, as Paul points out, but it was faithfully presented "according to" each of the four authors. This appeal to the four-fold Gospel shows that these Gospels were well known in the greater Church by the middle of the second century.

But there is the problem of differences and discrepancies among these Gospels. The words of Jesus are different and they appear in different contexts in different Gospels. One account of a miracle disagrees with another. To reconcile these differences, Tatian wrote a "harmony" of the four Gospels, the Diatesseron, which was read in the Syrian churches down to the fifth century. These kinds of harmonies which make one Gospel from the four continue to be published today. The correct view was that there was one Gospel in the four.

The touchstone or norm for acceptance of the Gospels and the other writings was the appeal to their apostolic origins. But, in practice, the basis of acceptance was the "rule of faith," a sense of what is "fit." The growth of this common consensus finally led to establishing the authentic collection, which, in turn, became the rule or measuring stick (canon) of Scripture. Latest to be accepted was Jude, the second and third Letters of John, II Peter, and, in the West, the Letter to the Hebrews because it was doubted that Paul himself wrote it. And the Apocalypse of John was resisted in many places because it gave rise to wild speculation and interpretations. It still does.

By the end of the fourth century, local councils in the East and in the West had basically the same collection of writings. The present writings of Scripture were solemnly confirmed at the Council of Trent.

And so, it took about three centuries to close the accepted list of writings, that is, to affirm a canon of Scripture. Closing the collection of texts opened it up to interpretation as, in some way, a unified whole. The expression New Testament, which originally meant new covenant (I Cor 11:25), or new relation between God and Israel sealed in the blood of Jesus, now became the term for the Christian writings which became a collection of texts that closed the Scripture.

(a) The Canon

The movement to define a collection of writings which expressed the identity of the Jewish people had already taken place after the destruction of Jerusalem. At the time of

Scripture Today

Jesus, there were different expressions of Judaism: the Saducees, associated with the Temple, the Pharisees, associated with popular religion, and the Essenes who shunned Temple worship because they claimed that the high-priests were illegitimate. But after the destruction of the Temple, the Pharisees became the voice of Judaism and sought to protect the authentic religion from the danger of contamination or even disintegration. Jamnia (or Javneh) is usually given as the place where a council was held to define the canon of Scripture (c. 90 A.D.). Actually, the process probably took place over a number of years. At any rate, the canon was defined as those writings in Hebrew up until the time of Ezra and nothing after. The need was for protection from outside threats, including that of the Christians.

The Christians, who had become more and more Greek-speaking, both Jews and Gentiles, had read the Scriptures in Greek, usually from the Greek translation of Alexandria called the Septuagint. In addition to some writings in Greek which were not translations from Hebrew, the sequence of books was somewhat different. The order was more open to a future fulfillment. The Talmud says that cursed be the day that the Scriptures were translated into Greek.

From the time of Luther, Protestant Bibles have followed the Hebrew canon for the Old Testament. Additions in the Greek translation of the Septuagint were relegated to what is called apochryphal writings. But in the Revised Standard Version they are included after the New Testament; and in the New English Bible they appear after the Old Testament.

John L. Boyle, S. J.

When we look at the writings of the New Testament, we see that the order is not historical. The correspondence of Paul was written first, but the Gospels come first because the source of the Gospel, as well as its center, is Jesus. Acts tells the story of the Gospel's spread. The Letters of Paul give directions for the growth of the churches in faith. The "Catholic Letters" are seen as addressed to the whole Church. And the Book of Revelation looks forward, in a time of persecution, to the final consummation. The Apocalypse of John is also a fitting ending to the Scripture because, through allusion, citation, and imagery, it recalls most of Scripture as being centered in Christ and the Church until the final coming of Jesus.

3) Some Observations on the Canon

The process to establish what is authoritative when faced with problems from within and without says as much about the nature of the Church as it does about the canon of Scripture. The use of these writings came about before their official approval. Of the various religious writings of the time, some were accepted and some rejected. Some were in doubt because of their use by the heretics, but later accepted. The norm given was apostolic witness: They somehow must reflect the historical beginnings. Christianity is not a timeless philosophy; it has its origin in an historical event and in a historical person. And this event and person came at the "fullness of time," the culminating act of God's action in the history of Israel; indeed, its beginning was creation itself. Hence, the need to preserve the authentic expression of this salvation history expressed in the tradition of Scripture.

But the determining factor in accepting the writings was always the norm of faith: what expressed the faith as the faithful knew and experienced it. Some religious writings which expressed the faith well were dropped because they didn't have a claim on apostolic witness. A few others were accepted which didn't seem too important because they did have this apostolic imprint. But the determining factor was the rule of faith. The canon formed by closing this collection then became, in turn, the norm of faith.

A final observation: the attempt to harmonize or homogenize the Gospel was rejected. The Gospel was according to one or another witness. Different witnesses to the Gospel tradition presented not an embarrassment but a richness. And the assimilation of this "word of the Lord" by Christians was meant to be manifest also in their witness, rooted in the witness of Jesus, a witness, for many, made in their blood.

IV. SCRIPTURE IN THE FATHERS

IN THE New Testament Christ is presented as the fulfillment of God's promise and the people's hope. But faith in this present reality of Christ and his Church is the ground of hope for the future completion which calls forth a living of the Gospel in mutual love to "build up" this present temple of God's presence until its completion.

Some images and symbols of this hope in the Old and New Testaments are the temple, Jerusalem, and the marriage-union between God and Israel. These images will be constantly reflected on and developed in the time of the Fathers.

The temple of old was the sign of hope for the new temple of the future (cf. Ezek and Zech). Paul says that we are that temple of living stones (I Cor 3:16). His mission and that of the community is to build up this present reality in love until the heavenly building or temple enfolds us. "For now we see in a mirror dimly, but then face to face. Now I know in part; then I shall recognize fully, as I have been recognized" (I Cor 13:12).

In presenting the allegory of the church as Jerusalem

Scripture Today

from above (Gal 4), Paul identifies the Church as the future Jerusalem prophesied by Isaiah (Isa 66). The present Jerusalem which is the Church will become the future Jerusalem coming down from heaven as a bride (Rev 21:2).

The marriage imagery of the Old and New Testaments follows the same pattern. The covenant between the Lord and the people in the wilderness is the sign of a future marriage-covenant. "Therefore, behold, I will allure her, and bring her into the wilderness, and speak tenderly to her. . . . And in that day, says the Lord, you will call me, 'My Husband.' . . . I will betroth you to me in faithfulness; and you shall know the Lord" (Hos 2:14-20). Paul uses the same imagery when he says to the church at Corinth, ". . . I betrothed you to Christ to present you as a pure bride to her one husband" (II Cor 11:2). This wedding symbolism is applied to the individual Christians in the parable of the wise virgins who enter the marriage feast (Matt 25:1-13). The same symbol refers to the future Church in glory, the new Jerusalem adorned for her husband (Rev 21:2).

This use of symbol and imagery to show the unity of God's plan in history and in Scripture will be characteristic of the Patristic reading of Scripture. It situates the call to discipleship in past, present, and future.

1) Two Tendencies

In the period of the Fathers, the Old and New Testaments were read as related one to the other. But there were two dif-

John L. Boyle, S. J.

ferent tendencies which appeared early and would continue throughout a millenium. The first method of interpretation had its origin in Alexandria. It would be countered by a school of interpretation centered in Antioch.

Alexandria was a strong center of Jewish thought represented by Philo, a leading Jewish exegete. He interpreted the historical events of Scripture through allegory. These events were to be read as examples of virtue leading to true wisdom: a life according to God's will. Pagan writers in Alexandria had already read the classic epic poems in this way.

The great representative of Alexandrian Christian exegesis was Origen who sought to see in all of Scripture the presence of Christ. Embarrassing statements or events, contradictions, unworthy human traits attributed to God were to be interpreted spiritually. For Origen, Jesus is the center of history and the fullness of Scripture. All of the Old Testament, both words and deeds, contributed to his coming; all has its true meaning only in him. Even obscure details and insignificant gestures take on a fuller and truer meaning in Christ. The literal sense, what happened then or what was expressed then, merely prepares the way for the truer spiritual sense.

Reacting to this minimizing of the literal sense of Scripture, the school of Antioch stressed the importance of the concrete events of history and the meaning of the original author. They saw that the allegorical approach of Alexandria, besides being arbitrary and fanciful, largely ignored the reality of history.

For example, Zech 9:9 says: "Rejoice greatly, O daughter of Zion! Shout aloud, O daughter of Jerusalem! Lo, your king comes to you; triumphant and victorious is he, humble and riding on an ass, on a colt, the foal of an ass." This text is referred to in all four Gospels at the entrance of Jesus into Jerusalem. In the literal sense, the text refers to Zerubabel, the Davidic ruler; but Origen stresses that in its truer, spiritual meaning it refers to Jesus. Theodore, from Antioch, claims that the prophecy does not have a double sense; it refers simply to Zerubabel. However, there are certain presentiments and vague hopes which are open to a future Messiah. He saw this openness to the future in prophetic texts not in a prophetic vision of the future Jesus but in the hyperbole of language. We would say the metaphorical and symbolic character of language.

For Theodore, the hopes of the prophets looked forward to a future fulfillment which they could not comprehend; but in this, God prepared the people for the coming of Christ.

A good example of the two approaches is in two different interpretations of the Third Psalm. The introduction to the Psalm says that it is a Psalm of David when he fled from Absalom, his son. And both Origen and Theodore take this for granted.

"O Lord, how many are my foes! Many rise against me.

John L. Boyle, S. J.

... I cry aloud to the Lord, and he answers from his holy hill.
I lie down and sleep; I wake again, for the Lord sustains me.''

Theodore tries to experience the soul of David who hopes in God in his own trial and expresses the hope of the people looking to the future. For Origen, the psalm is the prayer of David in its literal sense. But in its spiritual sense it is the prayer of Jesus who is rescued from death in the Resurrection. ''I lie down and sleep; I wake again for the Lord sustains me.''

Theodore tries to give each event in history, each past experience, each written expression, its own proper meaning. Each episode in the Old Testament has its own significance. There is an announcing of the Christ's coming in the prophetic vision of the future, but it does not yet signify it; it merely prepares for it. This preserves the concreteness of history and the originality of the authors of the Old Testament.

Origen sees the mystery of Christ present in the whole of history. He sees history as a whole and less in its parts. The meaning of earlier episodes can only be seen in their goal. Whereas Theodore focuses on the history of God's acts, Origen emphasizes the nature of God's activity. Theodore searches for the significance of an event in its precise historical context. Origen seeks the meaning which gives access to the mystery of Christ. For Theodore the key figure of the Old Testament is David, who, as prophet, looks to the future of history. For Origen, it is Moses, the seer, who experiences in the present the glory of the eternal God.

Some say that the differences between these two approaches stem from the different philosophies of each school. Alexandria represents Plato for whom the true reality is eternal. Antioch reflects Aristotle for whom reality is in concrete material history.

While it is true that each approach was influenced by the prevalent philosophy of each city, the different emphases in a theology of the Incarnation played a greater role. The tendency of Alexandria to stress the Eternal Word incarnate led to the heresy in which the divinity of Jesus virtually swallowed up his humanity. In the approach of Antioch, the humanity of Jesus remains fully intact; history retains its own autonomy. But the humanity is united to the divine in a "moral" way. That this kind of union of history and humanity with the eternal God is not quite enough was affirmed in the early Councils. These two tendencies in Scripture and in the Christological disputes of that time can still be seen in two approaches to Christology today: "from above" or "from below."

The reason for spending time on these two tendencies which emphasize the literal or the spiritual sense is that they continued throughout the period of the Fathers and Scholastic Theology. Indeed, they show up in interesting ways in more recent times. Perhaps it is due to the nature of the mystery of the Incarnation.

John L. Boyle, S. J.

The Fathers of the Church tried to keep a balance but the tendency to fanciful allegory was always present, especially when presented with obscure or embarrassing texts. When Jacob tells his blind father, Isaac, that he is really Esau, Augustine comments that this is not a lie; it's a mystery. Augustine also tries to extract hidden meanings from numbers when the context doesn't seem to justify it. Still, Augustine is quite right in seeing in the Samaritan woman who comes to the well of Jacob (John 4) a representative figure. Augustine says that she is a symbol of the reality but, as symbol, she becomes the reality in the time of the Church.

In the Old Testament, the New lies hidden; in the New Testament, the Old becomes clear. This principle of the Patristic period was reaffirmed in the document on the Word of God at Vatican II. It is illustrated in Augustine's comments on the Psalms and on the Our Father. He recommends that we pray the Psalms recognizing the union of Christ and the Church. Now one voice, now the other comes to the fore in our prayer. This Christological view is represented in the presentation of the Psalms in the Divine Office. These prayers which were composed at various times and in various circumstances were gathered together as one and are still prayed as the prayer of the Church united to Christ. Augustine also says that the petitions that Jesus tells us to pray in the Our Father are already present in the Old Testament. We can use these and be praying the Lord's prayer. "The one who says 'guide my ways according to your word and do not let iniquity rule over me' is saying: 'Your will be done on earth as in heaven'.''

2) The Good Samaritan

The parable of the Good Samaritan is a good example of Patristic exegesis, of its merits and its excesses. For most of the Fathers, the Good Samaritan is Jesus. It is not simply a parable told by Jesus which sheds light on the great commandment: love God wholeheartedly and your neighbor as yourself; it is a parable which explains the reality of the Christ-event, the center of the Gospel. It is the story of redemption.

In this approach, the story does not say that someone went down to Jericho, but that man (*anthropos*) goes down which, elsewhere, refers to humanity. Going down from a higher place (paradise or Jerusalem on high), humanity goes down, wounded by sin and left half-dead. The Jewish institutions do not save humanity. But Christ goes down on his way and, moved with pity, rescues fallen humanity. He bound up his wounds, pouring on oil and wine (Luke 10:34). Oil and wine refer to the remedies against sin and death (or they can refer to various other spiritual realities). ''He set him on his own beast.'' This refers to Jesus taking upon himself our infirmities as the Suffering Servant (Isa 53). He is the shepherd who puts the stray sheep on his own

49

shoulders (Luke 15:5). The inn is the Church; the two coins given to the innkeeper are the sacraments; and the return of the Samaritan will take place at the second coming. The command of Jesus at the end of the parable: "Go and do likewise" is another way of saying, "Love one another (even your enemies) as I have loved you."

Fanciful allegory is prevalent. The robbers, the beast, oil and wine, the two denarii are given specific meanings, though the meanings keep changing from one interpretation to another. This makes no difference. There is no attempt to quarrel with or refute any of these allegorical details. Popular etymology from the Hebrew root-meaning of words is also popular. Jericho comes from the Hebrew word for moon, which is changeable and from fullness begins to wane. Samaritan is from the word "watch over," as "he who watches over Israel." The tense of the verb "to go down" is also important. It is imperfect; which means that this is an abiding condition of humanity.

The story, then, tells of our redemption: Jesus has come to take upon himself our mortal condition to fulfill the Law and the prophets, to do the will of God and break down the wall of separation between Jew and Gentile. What this type of exegesis does is to focus on the central message of the Gospel. What it ignores is the simple but startling point of the parable that a despised outsider, the non-neighbor within Israel, is the one who does what the central commandment is all about.

It is justly said that this kind of exegesis misses the point of the parable in trying to recognize Jesus as the Samaritan. Which is true. However, when the reaction of the Samaritan is given ("He was moved with pity") the attentive reader/listener would recall that this earlier in the Gospel was used for Jesus when he saw the bereaved widow (Luke 7:13). In brief, Patristic exegesis is better at the whole picture but much weaker on the individual parts of the Gospel.

3) The Four-Fold Sense

We have seen how basic symbols and themes are taken up in the New Testament and seen in the past, present, and future. Patristic exegesis sees the message or call addressed to the reader/listener in Scripture as situated in this same context. Someone in the Middle Ages, reflecting on this way of reading Scripture, wrote: *littera gesta docet, quid credas allegoria moralis quid agas, quo tendis anagogia.* Roughly translated: the literal (sense) teaches the acts (of God); what you believe is allegory; the moral (sense), what you should do; where you are tending: anagogy.

The four senses are the first and last words of each line. But they have caused some confusion. The literal sense of Scripture refers to God's acts (*gesta*) in history and the original experience and expression in writing of this. It is sometimes called the historical sense; but it is not a positivistic view of history (what historians can discover of the past). It is the original experience of "the finger of God" in

51

human affairs, especially in the history of Israel. But in referring to the original experience of this, it can refer to the original intent of the author. The second part says that what you believe is allegory. This, too, is ambiguous. A better term is Christological: what the Scripture means in terms of Christ; how God's presence in human events enters history in a definitive way in the Christ-event. The moral sense is what each of us is called to do or feel, in act or in attitude; it is the call to a deeper following of Christ. And the last sense, anagogy, is where we tend, where we are meant to be going —full union with God.

The literal sense normally meant the acts of God leading up to the mystery of Christ and the Church and the faith of Christ (the second sense). But God's acts are meant to be continued in our lives. The moral sense is how we are to be open to God's action. *Gesta gestienda* is a phrase which was used. God's action should be continued in our lives. The literal sense is made literal through our living out our union with Christ. For the Fathers, the four senses are aspects of our reality.

For instance, Jesus in the Sermon on the Mount points out that he has come to fulfill the Law and the prophets. He says that the exterior precepts are meant to find a center in the human heart. This is the new covenant. And they must be lived. But the many external precepts of the Sinai-covenant were designed to enable the people of Israel to live in society, a society of a definite culture, legal system, and customary practices. Israel was a particular nation whose members were bound together by blood. When the new Israel, centered in Christ, is born, it is meant to break down the barriers between insider and outsider in a bond not of blood but of the Spirit. The code that Jesus gives is meant to transform society. But there are not a lot of exterior norms. We are to act like God: love your enemies. Jesus gives a general norm. But the particular example he gives for this is a "for instance." Walk the extra mile, turn the other cheek, give the stranger your cloak. Other ways of living the general norm are left to the freedom, the ingenuity, the imagination and discretion of the individual led by the Spirit of Christ. Martin of Tours gave away his cloak; Francis of Assisi gave up all his possessions. They understood Scripture by doing it literally. But there are still many other "for instances."

In spite of the many fanciful interpretations of the Fathers, the central interpretation of Scripture is not something left to the whim of the individual to explain, but it is a call to employ wit, wile, and willingness to bring about in our lives and in our world what Jesus is calling us to, what God is about in the world. In this sense, there are meant to be thousands, millions of interpretations.

The Fathers point out that the meaning of Scripture continues to change. But then they say that it is we who change, we who are called to grow by being open to the call in appreciation and generosity.

The invitation to prayer and the reading of Scripture in the monastic tradition was (and is) Psalm 95 with its warning against hardness of heart and a plea for an open and generous heart: "O that today you would hearken to his voice." (As the Letter to the Hebrews points out: this voice calls us today (Heb 4:7). And Ignatius of Loyola says that one reading the Gospels should enter with one's imagination into the story, as present to the scenes of the Gospel, and pray to be open to discern the call. This is the way to read/ listen to Scripture according to the Fathers.

(a) A Note on the Four-Fold Sense

It would be a mistake to see the formulation of a four-fold meaning as primarily a method for reading Scripture. It is basically an approach to the meaning of life. The mystery of Christ is seen as the focus which unites our past with our present living and future goal. And so, Scripture is read that way. Scripture is special because we encounter kindred spirits united by the one Spirit.

An example of the four-fold meaning today. A Marxist will interpret literature and the Bible, along with the visual arts, from the focus of dialectical materialism. History is viewed from that perspective and the future classless society is the goal. The literature or art reflects correct values or false, bourgeois attitudes. The correct reading of literature is meant to lead to practice, promoting the Cause. The four-fold meaning does not originate in a theory for reading literature. The method comes out of a world view.

It is the same with the Christian reading of Scripture during the Patristic period. But there is a difference. The historical event is already decisive: the Christ-event and the commitment to a living person, Jesus. However, this commitment is seen as weak or deficient. There is a constant call to a deeper conversion or further growth. And with a recognition of sinfulness, we do not see the enemy as simply "them." As Pogo in the old cartoon put it: "We have met the enemy and they are us." This call to further growth is the reason the Fathers say that the meaning of Scripture changes; it grows. It is not because the methodology for interpretation becomes better, but because the readers do. In the Fathers, the focus for reading Scripture is Christ, and the pre-condition, a desire for God.

4) Transition

This approach to Scripture was hardly critical; it left room for flights of fancy. But it was ordered to living. The centers of this interpretation can be considered the monasteries (this is put too simply, of course). But with the rise of the universities and a more critical, philosophical foundation for theology, a firmer foundation was demanded from Scripture. Only the literal sense, the original intent of the authors, could provide the basis for theological proof. St. Thomas Aquinas said: "Only the literal sense can be used for argument." The more traditional approach countered with: "The mystical meaning is not concerned with arguments." But with the rise of Scholastic Theology, a more reasonable ground for interpreting Scripture became prevalent (along with the more traditional reading).

The advantage is clear. Theology had a firmer foundation. Fanciful and arbitrary readings were minimized. A more critical approach, the literal sense, came to prevail. The disadvantage was that Scripture became a mine for extracting proof-texts to support a theological synthesis.

The literal sense in the Patristic tradition was mainly a springboard to the spiritual meaning. The sense of history was lost in any of its details; and so was the literary sense of Scripture. The Gospels (except for John) were largely homogenized; the particular, literary stamp of each author was missed. All of the prophets had the same style. But this was true also for those who championed the literal sense. Texts were searched for what presented clear statements on the truths of the faith. The artistic, affective, and symbolic expressions were minimized. It was not until a later age that the literary sense of Scripture would come into its own.

The aim of Scholastic Theology was "faith seeing understanding." This was also true of the Fathers; but "understanding" was meant in a more biblical sense: a recognition that comes from living the faith. We might put it: "faith seeking wisdom."

V. BEHIND SCRIPTURE

1) The Rise of Historical Exegesis

(a) The Renaissance

This renewal was occasioned by a re-discovery of ancient pagan literature: Latin and Greek. This recognition of a lost heritage developed into an exciting new humanism which influenced painting, sculpture, and literature. The *Divina Commedia* is profoundly Christian but it shows Dante's hommage to Virgil, as Virgil showed his dependence on Homer. In spite of worries that this paganism would undermine the faith, the Renaissance changed the method and content of education, one which has lasted until recent time: a classical education grounded in Latin and Greek. The growth in Renaissance humanism and the place of reason in the schools would profoundly affect the interpretation of Scripture, but this would not have its effect until some time later.

The event which had a greater influence on that change

was the Reformation. The Council of Trent would solemnly define the canon of Scripture because Luther had eliminated from the Old Testament those books written in Greek. He had also demoted some books of the New Testament. But more important than the difference in the canon, was Luther's stricture against a scholastic system of presenting the faith and his championing a return to Scripture alone. This would influence the history of interpretation in ways that Luther could scarcely perceive. A later, purely historical approach would have caused him great dismay.

The age of exploration and colonization had revealed a new world with peoples of different language, culture, and religion. And research into the past had opened up a world of the Near East out of which Scripture had emerged. The use of a positive, rational approach to the study of this past was, of course, all to the good. But in shunning dogmatism, some exegetes had pursued this quest with their own presuppositions of history which were bound to affect the results of their historical and literary investigations.

A few remarks on how we have obviously benefitted from this scholarship before getting into some problematic areas. A better investigation of the Hebrew language in the light of other languages of the Near East led to the surprise that this language was much different from the other "sacred" languages of Latin and Greek and, at the same time, more like the other languages of the Near East. It came to be recognized that Hebrew is just another Canaanite dialect. But with a wider literature to compare it with, better grammars and dictionaries were developed which, along with a better textual tradition, have given us better translations.

(b) Some Translations

A couple of examples can be cited on the meaning of common expressions in the Bible. We sometimes say that we desire God's mercy, not God's justice. This doesn't make much sense in terms of the way this word is used in Scripture. In Isaiah, especially the latter part, salvation is equivalent to God's justice, it flows from God's mercy and a fidelity to the promise. Familial relations of love are part of a just family relationship. God's choice of a covenanted people is the "just" relationship he chose. It does not mean what one has coming—one's just desserts. After sin and infidelity, Israel sought a renewal of this relationship of "justice," not because she deserved it but because God is faithful to his promises. So that this notion would not be confused with our ordinary legal meaning of justice, this word is often translated as "righteousness." This prevents a misinterpretation but has the disadvantage of meaning just about anything. We often consider an active concern for the poor to be works of charity. In a biblical perspective, it is seeking justice.

Discoveries of manuscripts and their relationship have also given more reliable texts for our translations. The Protestant ending to the Our Father from the King James version has "for thine is the kingdom," etc. The Catholic version doesn't have this ending. Most text critics now realize that this ending came from a liturgical expansion in the early Church. And so, the Revised Standard Version drops it from the text and Catholics have re-introduced it into the Liturgy.

At Christmas, we hear "Peace on earth, good will to men," but the Catholic version was ". . . to men of good will." Is "good will" genitive or nominative? Text critics would now say that the genitive is correct: "of good will," but it is God's good will or favor. And so, modern translations, whether Protestant or Catholic, translate it something like: "Peace on earth to those of God's favor."

A brief, historical overview is necessary to show how we got to where we are today in biblical studies. For convenience, we will consider Old Testament research first, and then studies in the New Testament.

2) Old Testament

In an age of scientific investigation, there was a natural conflict between rationalism and orthodoxy, religious commitment and honest scholarship. Advances were made in the scientific study of the text: philology, geography, types of literature. But it became clear that the people of the Old Testament were not rationalists. One approach to the Bible, then, as word of God, was that the Bible contains human words used at a certain time behind which was the word of

Scripture Today

God. With the development of human consciousness, many expressions have become outdated. They are only the shell of what is basic. One could feel free to pick and choose what was helpful or not for moral development. The Bible was a kind of smorgasbord. One chose what was helpful on the basis of personal inclination. This approach is still attractive today.

A reaction to a rationalistic, intellectual approach to Scripture came in the latter half of the eighteenth century, the Age of Romanticism, which emphasized feeling, affectivity, aesthetic sensitivity. This was the approach to literature in general, and it influenced the approach to the Bible. Two names associated with this approach are Lowth in England and Herder in Germany. Herder wrote on Genesis but was soon drawn to a study of the Psalms as poetry, the Bible as literature. The importance of this movement was that it would influence a study of the forms of the Psalms a century later by Gunkel. This would later influence the study of the forms of the Gospels. And the approach to the study of the Bible as literature is current among contemporary exegetes. Herder's view of the historical Jesus would also be picked up in a later, liberal approach to a kind of biography of Jesus. For Herder, Jesus showed the fullness of an immanent human spirit; his sensitivity was refined.

Strangely enough, this romantic spirit would lead to a more appreciative approach to the people of the Bible. They were no longer looked upon as benighted, lacking a reasonable approach to life.

John L. Boyle, S. J.

The emphasis on a critical, historical approach to Scripture had two interests: the literary sources behind the text and the history behind the text.

Already in the seventeenth century, Richard Simon (1638-1712), a French Oratorian, had noticed in the Pentateuch a difference in the use of the divine names. He posited two sources behind the present text. For this, he was attacked by Bossuet and his book finally placed on the Index. But later studies confirmed his observations; there were sources behind the Law of Moses. Later, an hypothesis was proposed by Wellhausen (1844-1918) that four written sources from different historical periods were behind the Pentateuch, not prior to Moses, but later, at a period covering almost five centuries from the ninth to the fifth centuries B.C. He called the first two sources Y and E for the different divine names Yahweh and Elohim, D for Deuteronomy, the basis of the Deuteronomic history from Joshuah to the end of Kings, and P for the priestly account, finished after the exile and emphasizing worship.

He surmised that a sixth book was part of this collection since the first two sources looked forward to the possession of the land. But the approach of Deuteronomy had taken over this period of history. Hence the term: Tetrateuch (four books), followed by Deuteronomy and Deuteronomic history.

The interest in written sources behind the text would continue in the investigation of the Gospels. Some drawbacks in Wellhausen's approach were a study of the history of Israel in isolation from the rest of the Near East, as well as a view of history as natural evolution. A gradual development from natural religion to a deeper moral sense was claimed for the prophets: the center of the religious history of Israel. Their moral stance was thought to be opposed to legal and cultic religion. This was later shown to be simplistic.

The gradual development of the present text of Isaiah was also pointed out: the first part (1-39) before the exile, the second (40-55) during the exile, and the third (56-66) after the exile. Emphasis was on the history and literature behind Scripture.

With the discovery of other literature from the Near East, emphasis shifted from a study of the history of the religion of Israel to that of the history of religions. The religion of Israel was one among others of the same region. This approach to Religious Studies is common in universities today. But the recognition of resemblances between religions proved fruitful in setting the context of Israel in a wider world of literature as well as history. We have mentioned Gunkel and his form criticism of the Psalms earlier. He emphasized the living situation of Israel behind the Psalms. This was an oral tradition later expressed in literary form. This view would be the basis of the study of various forms behind the Gospels. A Scandinavian approach would emphasize oral tradition as well as the centrality of worship and cult in the development and handing down of tradition.

The general approach to understand the history behind the text before the monarchy was skepticism. The writers were reliable only for the contemporaneous events. However, another approach, emphasizing archaeological finds, would try to show that there is a historical nucleus behind the narratives of the Pentateuch.

Perhaps a more important discovery in the study of the history behind the texts is the recognition of the Hebrew conception of history. After all, among the nations of the Near East, they were the first to take history seriously. But for them, it was the experience of God's actions for his people. Recalling these events, especially in a memorial celebration, was crucial both for their continued fidelity to God and the awareness of who they were as a people. Forgetting the past was the basic source of infidelity. The memorial celebration of the main festivals made the past present. It also made the people who they were.

In short, to the question: What's behind the Scripture of the Old Testament?, one answer is: The witness of the faith of a people who believed that God was present in their history of a lowly people set apart. They believed that God would be faithful in spite of their infidelity. Even though they felt powerless, God would lead them to their final goal.

3) New Testament

Scholarly research of the New Testament in many ways was different from that of the Old Testament. It is only one-fourth the size of the Old Testament and written in one-tenth the time. The main part was written in a little over fifty years. And it could be situated in a definite, well-known period of history. More importantly, the focus of research was on the person of Jesus. There was no search for the historical Moses in Old Testament research.

The first historical study of the New Testament was to situate it in Church history. Through the lens of Hegel, this history was viewed as a conflict between Jewish and Gentile Christianity or between the followers of Peter and those of Paul. Various syntheses were proposed.

For the historical order of the New Testament writings, the Letters of Paul were recognized as having been written first. And some kind of source(s) ante-dated the four Gospels.

At first, Mark was considered to be the last of the first three Gospels, and, essentially a digest of the other two (Griesbach: 1774). Then it was proposed that each depended on a form of an earlier Aramaic Gospel. Then, Mark was argued to be the first Gospel; only this could explain the absence of so much material. Herder claimed that Mark best preserved the oral Gospel which came first. Other studies claimed there were three oral Gospels, each behind the three Synoptics. Later study (Lachman: 1830) observed that where the narrative material in Matthew and Luke agree, they also agree with Mark. This pointed to Markan priority.

A recognition of material common to Matthew and Luke (mostly sayings of Jesus) was recognized as a source. It was simply referred to as the source: *Quelle* in German, short-

John L. Boyle, S. J.

ened to Q. This two-source theory of what's behind the Synoptic Gospels was generally accepted. But in the passage of time, different sources were postulated prior to these. This was not unlike the movement toward fragmentation in the source criticism of the Old Testament.

What was more characteristic of Gospel research was an interest in the historical Jesus. But there was skepticism about the possibility of discovering what Jesus was truly like because of the supernaturalism in the Gospels. Attempts at describing the life of Jesus tended to reflect the inclinations of the investigator. Jesus showed a developed sensitivity, or he was a social reformer, or a personal moralist, or a believer in the infinite worth of the individual and the brotherhood of man. To some, even if Jesus never existed, he is presented to us in the Gospels as an ideal.

Finally, Wrede (1901) pointed out that all of this was a reading into the Gospels. Even the idea of the messiahship of Jesus to be kept secret was a statement of faith of the early Church. A. Schweizer (1906) reviewed a century of research into the life of Jesus and showed the errors in it. He claimed that the only valid historical approach was to situate Jesus in the time of late Jewish apocalyptic expectations. Jesus looked forward to the Kingdom of God.

Other studies focused on the New Testament environment: the Greco-Roman world, Jewish apocalyptic thought, Gnostic teaching, and the Aramaic background. More recently, the influence of the writings called the Dead Sea

Scripture Today

Scrolls has been shown to shed light on some expressions in the New Testament.

As source criticism sought to discover the documents behind the Gospels, research tried to get behind the written documents to oral tradition. The method was basically at hand from Old Testament research: form criticism. Independent units could be recognized by formal patterns which addressed the various needs within the community—their life situation. These were gathered together and joined in various ways in the Gospels. Therefore, behind the Gospels are written sources in which are contained smaller units reflecting the life situations of the various Christian communities. Behind these is the situation of Jesus in his actual earthly ministry.

Finally, the attention of scholars was directed to the finished Gospels. They recognized that the final author was not merely a collector of traditions, but one who shaped, or edited that tradition with a particular stamp, a personal religious view, a special approach. This interest in the final form of the Gospel rather than the tradition behind it was called redaction or "editorial" criticism.

But between the interest in form and redaction criticisms, there was a renewed concern for understanding the Jesus behind the Gospels. This renewed quest for the historical Jesus is ably presented in the book in this series of Guidelines by Michael L. Cook, *The Historical Jesus*. He points out that the motivation behind this quest was theological

John L. Boyle, S. J.

rather than historical. Two opposing views in this search were those of Rudolph Bultmann and Joachim Jeremias. Though opposed to one another, the theological concerns of each came from a Lutheran perspective. Bultmann saw the attempt to look for the historical background of the Gospel as a use of reason to ground faith. This goes against the whole notion of faith as a gift of God. Faith can not be proved; and the object of faith is Christ and the Church, not the historical Jesus. Jeremias countered that the *kerygma* is the Church's response. The call of Jesus, not the response, is prior and decisive.

These positions and the response of others involved in the quest for the historical Jesus are admirably presented by Michael Cook in his book. But a few comments may be in order from a perspective found within the New Testament itself.

(a) A Note on the Historical Jesus

First of all, in answer to Jeremias, the New Testament, especially Paul, emphasizes that it is the response of Jesus that is decisive: his obedience even unto death. And to Bultmann, belief in the *kerygma* of the Church implies something about the historical Jesus. One requirement for someone to take the place of Judas and preach the *kerygma* was that he had been with Jesus from the beginning, i.e., from the preaching of John the Baptist. Clearly, they were not indifferent to the historical Jesus.

Scripture Today

More to the point: Bultmann presents Christ and the Church as the object of faith. But the New Testament, expecially Paul, presents Christ and the Church more as the source of faith. The more appropriate expression for Jesus as object of faith is: "Jesus Christ is Lord to the glory of God the Father" (Phil 2:11). And the perspective of Christ at the deepest center of the faith of the Church is presented in historical terms. But that is Paul's view of history and not the contemporary view.

It is often said that Paul betrays little interest in the historical Jesus. Perhaps part of the reason is that the memories about Jesus were so present. But a more theological view of history itself was behind his view of the historical Jesus. His central view of history might seem to us quite negative: History is the story of generations being born and dying. Death reigned. A popular etymology of the word "human" in Latin makes the same wry observation: it comes from "humus," the ground. The womb is the tomb. It's just a matter of time. We are mortals, defined by death.

Paul sees this condition as related to sin through history: an estrangement from the living God. God's action to overcome this condition is centered in the death of Jesus at the fullness of time. For Paul, the historical Jesus is the mortal Jesus, defined in terms of his own death and its meaning: a victory over sin and death. It is the depth of his mortality, his history, which is communicated to us in our mortality, our history. "We have been engrafted into the very shape of his death . . . that we might live with a newness of life"

(Rom 6:5). That is why Paul can talk about his experience of carrying the "dying" of Christ and desiring to know Christ and the power of the resurrection which is a sharing in his sufferings (Phil 3:10).

For Paul, the historical Jesus is the mortal Jesus with everything that means. And it is precisely the nature of his mortality, his history, which is at the center of our mortality, our history.

VI. CATHOLIC REACTION

Catholic scholars were largely innocent of the historical-critical approach to Scripture. There were a number of reasons for this. There was suspicion of a newer approach which ignored tradition in the Church and smacked of Rationalism. The leading scholars were heterodox Lutherans. And there was a general prejudice in Rome against an intellectual movement north of the Alps, where the sky is cloudy and the light obscure. But a number of the Lutheran scholars had also met opposition in their own churches. Some were forced to leave their teaching positions.

At a time which exalted reason, Vatican I (1870) found it necessary to defend reason against the fideists who exalted faith over and against natural reason. Citing the teaching of Paul in the first part of Romans, the Council affirmed God's revelation in creation and added that prophecies and miracles in both the Old and New Testament periods were objective facts which should lead reasonable people to faith. The Second Vatican Council would emphasize a more traditional view that would emphasize not facts in history which should lead to faith but acts (*gesta*) of God in history discerned through faith.

1) Providentissimus Deus

Toward the end of the nineteenth century, Leo XIII faced the crucial need for Catholic scholarship in Scripture studies and the need for a deeper grounding in Scripture for the Church, especially in seminaries. His encyclical letter on Scripture *Providentissimus Deus* (1893) was part of a larger attempt at renewal within the Church and a more realistic entrance into the conditions and problems of the world. He had called for a renewal of a philosophical grounding of theology especially from a renewed study of St. Thomas Aquinas (1779). But he is best known for his social encyclical on the condition of the working class and the rights of laborers. This became the foundation for a tradition of encyclicals on the economic and social conditions of the world (*Rerum Novarum:* 1891).

The encyclical on Scripture was a cautious acceptance of the newer approaches to Scripture. In it, he praised M. J. Lagrange, O.P., a pioneer in the use of the critical methods of research and founder of the Dominican school of biblical research in Jerusalem, the *Ecole Biblique.* Lagrange had already expressed the indebtedness of the Church to non-Catholic scholars, especially the Germans, for their scholarship.

Scripture Today

The acceptance of the historical-critical method was cautious. It was shown in a two-pronged approach in the letter —defense of tradition, but openness to the new interpretation. Leo points out that historical investigations should be made into the origin and traditions of the writings of Scripture but warns against a purely positivistic approach to history alone. Against a naive literalism, he points out that the sacred writers did not intend to teach the natural things of the universe but "what is profitable for salvation." This would again be emphasized in Vatican II. He also said that the writers of ancient literature expressed themselves in the ordinary expressions of their time. Hence, the need for research to interpret the meaning of Scripture written in a different culture. There was also the obvious need to study the ancient languages of the Near East and of early manuscripts. He also recommended the importance of employing the findings of non-Catholic research, with prudence.

To promote this renewal in Scriptural studies, he formed the Biblical Commission (1902) which should both promote a deeper interpretation of Scripture but also defend against every error or dangerous opinion.

Pius X worked to implement this program. He established norms for academic degrees in Scripture conferred by the Biblical Commission. He outlined a plan for courses in Scripture throughout the period of studies in the seminary. And he urged again the study of ancient language, archaeology, geography, history, and theology. For this, he founded the Pontifical Biblical Institute in Rome. Unfortunately, this initial openness to new methodologies turned to wariness and suspicion. The cause was Modernism.

2) Modernism

Modernism was a general movement within Roman Catholicism, not a teaching. It sought to make the Church and Catholic belief more relevant to contemporary life: social, political, scientific, historical, and philosophical. The opinions of the Modernists were often at odds with one another but, in common, these tendencies were seen as an attack against tradition. Modernism was called the synthesis of all heresies. But since it was perceived as so pervasive and diffuse, the defense was a blanket condemnation of everything opposed to tradition. Since Modernism was more a climate than a teaching, the reaction to it was an atmosphere of fear and protection against a mortal danger.

In Scripture studies, Alfred Loisy is usually cited as an example of Modernist tendencies. He recognized the historical development of Scripture and that the Gospels reflected more the faith of the Church than an exact account of the historical time of Jesus. But he went on to deny the historicity of miracles and the consciousness that Jesus had of a special, divine relationship to God. He was excommunicated in 1908.

Examples of this defensive attitude of the Church can be seen in a decree (*Lamentabile:* 1907) condemning sixty-four propositions, many of them connected with Scripture. Even though the decree did not condemn the historical-critical method, it was certainly reactionary. But it is important to realize what is condemned and the nature of the condemnation. For instance, the proposition is condemned that the discourses contained in the Fourth Gospel ". . . are theological meditations, devoid of historical truth concerning the mystery of salvation." This does not mean that the discourses are not in any way theological meditations. And the nature of the condemnation is not specified. Are the propositions false or dangerous? Indeed, the approach focused more on the danger of the propositions than anything else.

3) *Divino Afflante Spiritu*

M. J. Lagrange had praised the encyclical of Leo XIII on Scripture as the *Magna Carta* of Catholic biblical scholarship. Fifty years later, other Catholic scholars would use the same expression for the encyclical of Pius XII. As Pius XI had shown that his social encyclical was in continuity with the social teaching of *Rerum Novarum* by calling it *Quadragesimo Anno* or the fourtieth year after, Pius XII issued his letter on Scripture on the golden jubilee of Leo's encyclical.

Two years earlier, an anonymous tractate was sent to bishops in Italy attacking the scientific study of Scripture. And so the encyclical was defensive; but this time, of the scientific research of the Bible. The letter was decidedly optimistic, though written during a terrible war. It encouraged Catholic scholars in research and affirmed the primacy of the literal sense of Scripture. Facing difficulties in interpreting the text, the exegete should use every help from research to determine the peculiar character and circumstance of the sacred writer, the age in which he lived, the sources which he used, written or oral, and the manner of expression he employed.

Pius pointed out that the literal sense is not that obvious in ancient literature. The interpreter must go back to those times and make use of the aids afforded by history, archaeology, and other literary records to discover what literary forms the writers used back then. And he condemned those in the Church who oppose anything new as suspect and contrary to tradition just because it was not said before. He added a reminder that there are very few passages in the Bible whose meaning has been defined by the Church or consistently interpreted by the Fathers.

With praise for biblical scholars and encouragement for those engaged in the study of Scripture, Pius XII gave a bigger boost to the Catholic biblical movement than anyone had in recent times.

4) Vatican II

The calling of Vatican II by Pope John XXIII took place when Catholic biblical research was once more under attack. The Biblical Institute, in particular, felt the brunt of the hostility when two professors were forbidden to teach without reasons given. An article appeared in an Italian theological journal denying that *Divino Afflante Spiritu* supported the newer trends in exegesis. One wonders if the author had actually read the encyclical. And this hostile attitude began to gain support. These views were translated and made available to the bishops at the beginning of the Council.

The first draft on the Sources of Revelation presented to the bishops showed signs of a step backward. It was defensive in tone and its categories were more dogmatic than scriptural. It never mentioned literary forms or development that went on before the final text of the Bible. There were no problems at all in the historicity of the Gospels. Anyone who called into question "the true historical and objective truth of the events of Jesus' life and the authenticity of his words" was condemned.

The view of Revelation was that of doctrine handed down by the two separate sources of Scripture and Tradition, with an emphasis on the latter. The majority of bishops voted to reject the document, and John XXIII ordered the document to be redone under another newly formed commission. The second draft emphasized salvation history as the manner of revelation, but the model was still that of doctrine handed down. Few were satisfied with the text this second time around.

While the third draft was being prepared, the Biblical

John L. Boyle, S. J.

Commission issued an instruction "On the Historical Truth of the Gospels." It encouraged the Catholic exegete to use the historical methods of form and redaction criticism. The Instruction wisely and clearly distinguished between the form-critical method itself and unwarranted and unacceptable pre-suppositions that had sometimes accompanied the use of this method in the past: denial of God's active presence in the world by revelation, denials of the possibility of miracles and prophecy, opposition between faith and historical truth, and an emphasis on the creative formulation of the community that would give no importance to apostolic witness.

But after mentioning these incorrect pre-suppositions, the Instruction pointed out the three stages in the transmission of the Jesus-tradition: the life-situation of Jesus himself, the life-situation of the churches, and the life-situation of the particular evangelist. The Instruction also noted the various forms of proclamation: e.g., catechesis, narrative, hymns, prayers, etc.

In explaining redaction criticism, the Instruction noted how each evangelist made use of the tradition in a way suitable to the special purpose he had in mind and the particular need of the church. This description of the Instruction was taken over and summarized in the final form approved by the Council:

The sacred writers [with a clearer understanding which they had in the light of the Resurrection and the Spirit of

78

truth] wrote the four Gospels, selecting some things from the many which had been handed down by word of mouth or in writing, reducing some of them to a synthesis, explicating some things in view of the situation of the churches, and preserving the form of proclamation, but always in such fashion that they told us the honest truth about Jesus. Cf. *Dei Verbum,* ch. 5, no. 19.

The Old Testament section (ch.4) repeats a principle of the Fathers that the New Testament is hidden in the Old and the Old made manifest in the New; but it also emphasizes the historical development of the Old Testament through Israel's growing experience of God and the ways of God.

More important in the development of the different drafts on Revelation was the movement toward the interrelationship between Scripture and Tradition, and of Revelation as a personal relationship to God in community. Tradition was no longer focused on doctrinal tradition but on the entire life of the Church. And revelation was God's self-disclosure in history which has as its goal this final interpersonal relationship with us. The form of revelation, or secondary object, is God's word, the witness through which God's act of self-giving is mediated. Experienced in a special way in Scripture, this tradition continues and develops in the Church through the activity of the Holy Spirit. First of all, "through the contemplation and study made by believers, who treasure these things in their hearts (Luke 2:19,51), through the intimate understanding of spiritual things they

John L. Boyle, S. J.

experience, and through the preaching of those who received through episcopal succession the sure gift of truth'' (*Dei Verbum,* ch. 2, no. 8).

An answer to the question: What's behind Scripture? might be: The community witness of those who have experienced God in personal faith centered in the fully expressed witness of Jesus.

VII. SCRIPTURE TODAY

1) The Bible as Literature

From the notion of the Gospel writers as editors of tradition, there followed a growing recognition that they were true authors. From a focus on those particular verses which were from the final writer and betrayed the particular interest and religious point of view, there dawned the realization that each Gospel should be approached as a unity in its entire composition with structure, rhythm, and imagery all forming a unity. The approach to Scripture most prevalent today, then, is literary. Each book of the Bible is not simply a collection of traditions of the past but a unified literary work. And so it should be approached with the methods of ordinary literary criticism.

It is interesting that this recognition came both from the side of those seeking the historical Jesus behind the sources (cf. Cook: *The Historical Jesus,* last chapter) but also from those investigating the growth in the tradition from oral tradition down to the final form of the Gospels. This convergence from two distinct points of view is remarkable. And in all areas of theology, the importance of the story, narratology, is being stressed.

A literary approach focuses on what is there in the text. The point of view is simple: literature should be read as literature. In literature different aspects are predominant. In a front page news article the referential aspect is emphasized —the event referred to. In other writings, the involvement of the writer by emotion or commitment is more important, or the mastery of presentation, or the various ways of involving the audience. And the point of view can be different: strong affirmation, tongue-in-cheek, irony, sarcasm, damning with faint praise. But any of these aspects should be present in the text. We cannot ask the author.

A Gospel is a piece of literature with story and speeches as part of the story. It is supposed to have an impact; and so devices of story-telling and rhetoric are chosen which will best have this effect. Although there is a history behind the Gospel story, the Gospel is not like a window which immediately opens our gaze to that history behind the text. It is not transparent to that history and is not meant to be. We are called to enter into the world of the story.

(a) The Story

In Mark's Gospel, Jesus is able to know the interior thoughts of friend and foe; he can read hearts. We might say that he is clairvoyant (although the author is calling to mind the Lord who, in Scripture, reads the heart). We seldom consider the fact that the narrator has even greater insight; he even knows the deepest thoughts and attitudes of Jesus. The narrator is omniscient. We hardly notice this because we are used to stories where the narrator knows all the secret thoughts and attitudes of the characters in the story. He even knows the future which is carefully hidden from the people in the story and from the readers until the proper moment. Even historians will tell us what Napoleon was thinking at the Battle of Waterloo. History is not simply facts and figures. Writing history in story form makes it more human.

Since Mark, the real author, didn't know what Jesus was thinking, the one in the text who does know is called the implied narrator. The one to whom the Gospel is directed is also implied from the text: the implied reader who is supposed to respond to the story in an appropriate way. As such, the implied reader is often called the ideal reader. A real reader might miss the point of the story. To appreciate the Gospel one must enter into the story and should respond in the right way to the performance of the reading. Until the story is read or performed, the Gospel is merely ink on paper.

(b) Some Examples

In the Lukan Passion account, there is a small section usually called the Denials of Peter because it shows how the prophecy of Jesus about Peter's denials is fulfilled. But it should be called the Conversion of Peter. In Matthew and Mark, after Peter maintains that he will never desert Jesus even though the others might, Jesus predicts that Peter will deny him. But in Luke, Jesus says, "Simon, Simon, behold Satan has tried to sift you [the apostles] as wheat, but I have prayed for you [Peter] that your faith may not fail; and when you have turned again, strengthen your brethren" (Luke 22: 31-32). It is only after this prayer for Peter's conversion that Jesus predicts the denials.

After Peter denies Jesus and the cock crows, the text says, ". . . the Lord turned and looked at Peter; and Peter remembered the word of the Lord . . . and went out and wept bitterly" (Luke 22:61-62). Out of nowhere we are told that the Lord (not Jesus) turned and looked at Peter. Even without knowing the significance of the phrase, we know that it must relate to Peter's conversion because that is what we have been prepared for. (The turning of the Lord is an expression in Isaiah and elsewhere to show God's initiative in conversion.) And the strange wording of the turning of the Lord suggests Peter's conversion as a paradigm for any conversion. The reader is supposed to identify in some way with the story. Commentaries that try to situate Jesus some place, either in the building or out in the courtyard, miss the point.

Another example: also in Luke's Passion account, is the strange observation after the appearance of Jesus before

Scripture Today

Herod: "And Herod and Pilate became friends with each other that very day, for before this they had been at enmity with each other" (Luke 23:12). Details in the Passion account usually have some significance. This is the most theological section in all of the Gospels. To mention here the resumption of diplomatic relations between Herod and Pilate seems out of place. We are left wondering what this is all about. It's like a pebble in the shoe.

When the incident is recalled in Acts as a fulfillment of Scripture (Psalm 2), the tension is resolved. In Acts 4:23-31, the community recites in chorus Psalm 2: "Kings of the earth set themselves in array, and the rulers were gathered together, against the Lord and against his anointed." And then they continue their prayer: "For truly in this city were gathered together against your holy servant Jesus, whom you anointed, both Herod and Pontius Pilate, with the Gentiles and the people of Israel. . . ." We have already been prepared for this prayer which interprets Scripture in the light of the Christ-event by the strange mention of the friendship of Herod and Pilate. And this prayer also suggests that since both Gentiles and the peoples of Israel are involved in the death of Jesus, they are also both involved in the salvation that comes from it. This is a key theme of Luke-Acts.

Another example of suspense in one scene which sets up another scene is once again the denials of Peter, this time in the Gospel of John. In the other Gospels, the scene is set for the denials of Peter: fire or light; and then, the action of the denials. But in John's Gospel, Peter denies Jesus and then the scene is set: a charcoal fire. In a movie, if we see some action and then the camera moves in on a detail of the scene, we know that the detail will appear later. So also here. In the resurrection appearance to the disciples by the Sea of Tiberias, the disciples got out of the boat when they reached the shore. The text then says ". . . they saw a charcoal fire there. . ." (John 21:9). We have been prepared for the conversion scene with Peter. It has a greater impact.

Another strange scene in Matthew's Passion account is often called "The Death of Judas" because in it Judas hangs himself (Matt 27:3-10). But in the text it is a prelude to the appearance before Pilate. It is preceded by mentioning that they bound him and led him away and delivered him to Pilate the governor. Obviously, the author is not interested in a chronological sequence; and yet the scene is supposed to shed light on the Pilate episode. And, though Judas' suicide is mentioned, the emphasis is on the field. The key words in the scene are blood and money. A better paragraph heading would be "The Price of Blood."

A typical fulfillment text of Matthew is then cited: "Then was fulfilled what had been spoken by the prophet Jeremiah, saying, 'And they took the thirty pieces of silver, the price of him on whom a price had been set by some of the sons of Israel, and they gave them for the potters' field, as the Lord directed me'." The thirty pieces of silver is from

Zechariah and refers to the people's rejection of the Lord (Zech 11:13), but the quotation is said to come from Jeremiah. The emphasis is on the field of redemption (Jer 32:7). In Acts: 1:19, we find out that Haceldama, Field of Blood, was so called because of the untimely death of Judas. But in Matthew it is the blood of Jesus which is the price for the field of redemption, even through the rejection of the people.

It is by not seeing the essential literary connection between this scene of the field of redemption and the blood theme in the scene before Pilate that most commentaries miss the point of the strange expression: "The entire people answered, 'his blood be upon us and on our children'" (Matt 27:25). It is often cited as an anti-Jewish polemic of Matthew. (Actually, the only anti-Jewish reference in Matthew is: ". . . this story [the disciples stole the body] has been spread among the Jews to this day" (Matt 28:15). Often, a corrective is given that only the Jewish leaders were responsible. But, again, literarily, the character-group "the people" appears in this scene out of nowhere.

What is characteristic of this group comes out of the whole text of Matthew: "He will be called Jesus, for he will save the people from their sins" (Matt 1:21). And the blood theme that has prepared us for this scene is at the Last Supper: "this is my blood for the forgiveness of sins" (Matt 26:28). In Matthew, the people, Israel, has become the Church, the true Israel. To use the text to show that a group was responsible back then seems to merit Jesus' condemnation of the Scribes and Pharisees: "You say that if we had lived [back then] in the days of the prophets, we would not have been responsible for the blood of the prophets" (Matt 23:30).

A final example might be that of the "midnight streaker" in Mark's introduction to the Passion account. At the arrest of Jesus, all the disciples fled (Mark 14:50) as Jesus had predicted (Mark 14:27); but then comes a strange verse that says they laid hold of a young lad, a close follower of Jesus, with a linen cloth thrown around his naked body. He left behind the linen cloth and fled naked (Mark 14:51-52). This has sometimes been cited as an autobiographical reference, which would be odd to find here in the Passion account. It awakens puzzlement and interest. At the conclusion of the Passion, we are told that they bought a linen cloth and, taking Jesus down, they wrapped him in the linen cloth and laid him in a tomb (Mark 15:46). It is interesting that a linen cloth is mentioned twice in the introduction and twice in the conclusion.

As the three women enter the empty tomb on Sunday, the vision they have is that of a young lad "seated at the right (side? hand?) with a white robe thrown around him." He delivers the Easter message: "Do not be amazed; you seek Jesus of Nazareth, crucified. He has been raised up; he is not here; see the place where they laid him. But go tell his disciples and Peter [who had scattered and denied Jesus] that he goes before you [as he went before them to his Passion in Jerusalem] into Galilee. There you will see him as he told you" (when he foretold the scattering of the disciples and the denials of Peter in Mark 14:27-31).

The mention of a young lad only occurs in Mark at the introduction to the Passion and here as herald of the Resurrection. And a throw-around garment is mentioned in both places: there, a linen cloth; here, a white robe. If the writer knows how to write, there must be a connection. It must be a sign or symbol of something. The expression "seated at the right" is familiar and is usually translated "seated at the right hand" in other parts of the New Testament.

Clothing has a symbolic meaning in both Old and New Testaments. Paul reminds the church at Corinth: "We know that if the earthly tent we live in is destroyed, we have a building from God, a house not made with hands, eternal in the heavens. Here, indeed, we groan, and long to put on [as a garment] our heavenly dwelling so that by putting it on we may not be found naked. For while we are still in this tent, we sigh with anxiety; not that we would be unclothed (in death) but that we be further clothed, so that what is mortal may be swallowed up by life" (II Cor 5:1-4). Nakedness refers to death and the clothing from above is eternal life. The "white robe" of the young man would seem to have the same meaning as the white robe which clothes those who have gone through persecution and death and are now in glory (Rev 7:13-15).

John L. Boyle, S. J.

In short, the young lad is a sign of the victory over death in the Resurrection. In presenting him in the strange scene introducing the Passion account, our curiosity is piqued so that the vision at the tomb has a greater impact.

The approach taken in these examples is not based on any particular literary theory. It is merely an attempt to pay attention to the pointers in the text which shed light on the meaning of the text as we have it.

(c) Some Problems

The literary approach is an approach to any kind of literature. The examples given from the Gospels were all narrative. In using a kind of literary approach, I also used the Greek text here and there and made use of some observations which were more historical, or referred to other writings in the New Testament to try to understand some of the imagery. For some who espouse the literary approach to Scripture, this is cheating. Indeed, for some, to refer to the Greek text behind the English translation is improper. We should examine the text in front of us even though textual critics point out that it is a poor translation.

This pure literary approach seems excessive. The pendulum has gone too far to the other side. If a literary approach is a corrective to a historical-critical approach, it needs its own correction. First of all, some of it is excessively complicated for the amount of light it sheds on the text. Sec-

Scripture Today

ondly, examples chosen are usually from the literature of fiction and not from literature which is formed from previous sources and is part of a particular tradition. An approach to the poem "The Waste Land" by T.S. Eliot which is not grounded in the poetic tradition to which the poem alludes could hardly illuminate the text. And to appreciate the poem, the implied reader shares in that tradition. This is especially true of the Gospels.

A structuralist approach to Scripture concentrates on the text at hand and avoids historical issues. It criticizes past exegetes who were more concerned with history than with meaning. But in emphasizing the meaning within the text, it usually ignores any referent to a concrete, historical world. Structuralism can be a good preparation for interpretation, but it usually stops short of interpretation.

It might be good to recall a reference which the Letter to the Hebrews makes concerning what is behind Scripture. In chapter 11, the author recalls the great people of the past who witnessed to their faith, many by giving their lives. Christ and the Church are not simply the fulfillment of prophetic oracles and historical types; they are the fulfillment of the faithful lives of people who have gone before and have prepared for this reality at the fullness of time. "And all these, though well attested by their faith, did not receive what was promised, since God had foreseen something better for us, that apart from us they should not be made perfect" (Heb 11:39-40).

John L. Boyle, S. J.

In this first list of the communion of saints, this "cloud of witnesses," there are no Christians; but they are joined in communion with us. This is behind Scripture.

(d) The Reader in the Story

We are all familiar with the way Nathan, the prophet, involved his audience, David, in the story of the rich man who stole the lamb from the poor man. Involved in the story, David became angry and said the rich man deserves to die. With the trap sprung, Nathan points out: "You are the man" (2 Sam 12:1-7).

But there are other ways the story-teller involves the reader and then springs the trap. One is the more gentle trap of humor. Jonah is an unlikely prophet and a reluctant one; when told to head east to Niniveh, he flees west. He escapes from a storm through an unlikely fish that swallows him and then disgorges him on the shore to complete his mission. He preaches without enthusiasm but, surprisingly, the city is converted; all do penance, including the cattle. This incredible success greatly annoys Jonah. He takes refuge under a plant and pouts. The Lord dries up the plant and Jonah sulks all the more. We are left with the Lord poking poor Jonah in the ribs saying it is proper that he show mercy to these despised outsiders. The book ends with Jonah still sulking, a humorous and pathetic figure. And then, perhaps, we feel a nudge in the ribs ourselves.

Scripture Today

Jonah was written at a time when his attitude toward the Gentiles was characteristic. In the story, this attitude is not harshly condemned. It is presented in a wonderful story which holds it up to humorous ridicule.

It seems that something like this is also going on in Mark's Gospel in the depiction of the disciples. They are called to be disciples as we are. In the explanation of the parable of the sower, they are especially privileged. They are not like the outsiders to whom everything happens in riddles; to them is given the mystery of the Kingdom of God. We too are privileged; the explanation is given to us also. But in the next section that tells of the mission of the disciples, we find ourselves in a superior position. Twice they are told to feed the crowd; but they lack provisions. Nonetheless, they feed the crowd with bread left over. They don't recognize the presence of the Lord when they have difficulty crossing the sea. Without provisions of bread, they don't recognize the One Bread with them in the boat. They are rebuked by Jesus as being hard of heart for not remembering how the Lord had been present with them. They do not understand.

But we understand; until, perhaps, we hear a small voice ask, "Do you?" Written to a church in difficulty, experiencing few resources in a time of persecution, Mark's Gospel story is a message of hope. But the tender trap is to set up the readers/listeners to feel superior to the disciples before they recognize that the story is their story, our story.

John L. Boyle, S. J.

This literary approach to a section of Mark's Gospel shows a strategy for involving the audience in the story. But it also converges with the point made in the first chapter on Gospel. What kind of literature is Gospel literature? What is the effect of drawing the traditions of the Jesus-story into the genre of Gospel?

2) The Story in the Story

Any section of Scripture is set in a wider context; one chapter of a book has its full meaning in terms of the whole. In the past, Isaiah was divided into three sections based on what period it came from. And in some commentaries Isa 40-66 is set apart from Isa 1-39 by other books of the Bible which were, presumably, written at the same time. But this approach has drawbacks. There are oracles in the first part of Isaiah given at the time of the Assyrian power; others are pronounced against the Babylonians. And chapters 24-27, the Isaian Apocalypse, are considered to have been written last of all. The attempt to divide Isaiah into historical units cannot be consistently followed. Besides, it tends to atomize the text. We are being constantly reminded that one section or another is an addition.

It is better to consider the text of Isaiah as one (although it probably took over two centuries to reach its present form). Some scholars have pointed out the development and

Scripture Today

unity of symbolism in the final text. This means that the symbolism of the first part develops its significance and meaning in the wider context of the whole of Isaiah.

We pointed out earlier how investigations into the sources behind the Pentateuch revealed four of them (at least). And the earliest sources must have had some account of the conquest of the land. This is behind the notion of the hexateuch. But what we have is the Pentateuch, the foundational document of Israel—the Law. At the end of the Pentateuch, we find Israel still looking eagerly with hope to enter into the promised inheritance. This was the experience of Israel even after the return from exile. They experienced that they were exiles in their own land. The spiritual "Deep River" expresses this feeling very well—the desire to cross over into "camp ground." These people who were recently slaves but still outsiders in their land caught the feeling of the Pentateuch better than the source critics.

And since the Lord predicted the exile already in Deuteronomy, the books from Joshua to Kings were not so much the story of how we won the West, as it was how we lost the Land. This also explains why the most important festivals, as well as basic themes in the prophets and psalms, recalled the period in the desert and not the conquest of the land. This becomes clearer when we accept the Old Testament in its present form and its wider context.

Psalm 22 is called a psalm of lament by a suffering just one, but it ends on a triumphant note of thanksgiving. The

John L. Boyle, S. J.

Psalmist, in great danger, prays for deliverance. He recalls the saving presence of the Lord in the history of the people and in his own life. This "memory" of the past, so central to the religion of Israel, is the basis for his strong hope of deliverance. But then the tone changes in verse 27. His deliverance has a universal significance. This section is often called an addition. But the addition colors the meaning of the whole psalm. It is not simply tacked on.

And a Christian praying: "My God, my God, why have you forsaken me?" could not help recalling the prayer of Jesus on the cross. This is its wider context.

John Ciardi explains, in his introduction to poetry, *How Does the Poem Mean?,* that verses in a good poem are like a stone thrown into a pond that sets up ripples in all directions. What is true of good poetry is also true of many parts of Scripture. But it is important to maintain, first of all, the psalm, or oracle, or narrative in its concrete, individual, historical setting. We have seen how the tendency of Alexandria was to see the parts of Scripture always in terms of the whole. The tendency of Antioch was to preserve the concrete, historial setting of each of the parts. The balance between the two is always difficult. What follows is an attempt to appreciate the story of "the binding of Isaac" as narrative, but then set it in its ever widening context.

God tested Abraham (Gen 22) by telling him to sacrifice his only, beloved son on a chosen mountain in the land of Moriah. We go with Abraham on this journey of faith. Told

Scripture Today

first of all to abandon his past (Gen 12), he is now called to abandon his future, to hand over his beloved son to death. We share the wonder of Abraham at the mystery of this God to whom he has committed his life. We see the place of the mountain with the eyes of Abraham. At the last moment, Abraham responds: "Here am I" to the angel who comes to stay his hand (Gen 22:11), the same willing response he gave to God at the beginning (Gen 22:1). We are still in wonder of the God of Abraham. But then the angel focuses attention on the faith of Abraham which is a model for Israel and a source of blessing even for all the nations of the earth.

This story is set in the wider story of Abraham; but it is remembered again in the story of the Temple, said to be built precisely at this spot on Mount Moriah (2 Chron 3:1). The faith of Abraham is the foundation for true religion and the true worship of Israel. Even in the original story, the name which Abraham gives for the mountain ("God Will Be Seen") is a phrase used for temple worship.

But there is a wider context. Paul recalls the story when he says: "He who did not spare his own Son but gave him up for us all, will he not also give us all things with him?" (Rom 8:32). And in the Gospel of John we hear that the ultimate basis for our call to be born from above as children of God is: "God so loved the world that he gave his only son" (John 3:16). To appreciate the meaning of Paul and John, we are called to "remember" the story of Abraham.

John L. Boyle, S. J.

But now the basis of true religion is not so much the faith of Abraham as it is the love of this mysterious God of Abraham, the God and Father of our Lord, Jesus Christ. In reading the New Testament, we remember the Old. And in reading the Old, we are aware of a wider context of meaning.

3) A Wider Context

The document on Revelation and Scripture in Vatican II should also be seen in the wider context of other documents of Vatican II. We are conscious of the important role of Scripture in the document on the Liturgy. From this document have come the new Lectionary of readings for the Eucharist and other liturgical celebrations. The context of Liturgy gives us the privileged location for reading/listening to Scripture where the Church in "remembering" makes the event of Christ and the Church present; she expresses her true identity. The Lord is present in the Church in her faith, in the proclamation of faith, and as our physical food and drink. This should always be remembered in our private reading of Scripture.

But there is also a wider context emphasized in the document "On the Church in the Modern World." We are called to continually widen the horizon of our lives in recognizing more deeply the true world in which we live, not the world of advertisements. This will continually influence the way

Scripture Today

we read Scripture, as Scripture should continually influence our vision of life.

Sounds of people shouting, horns blaring, and a general clamor fill the chapel of the Sisters of Charity in a poor section of Calcutta during the reading of Scripture and the celebration of the Liturgy. Some, working there with Mother Teresa, found this "background music" distracting at first; but then it became the proper and wider context.

VIII. CONCLUSION

The last chapter emphasized a contemporary reading of Scripture which is literary. Other important studies emphasize the sociological background of Israel and the early Church, as well as the importance of the canon in biblical interpretation. And Cook in his last chapter of *The Historical Jesus* emphasizes the perspective of various liberation movements.

A number of signs of hope come to mind in forecasting the future of Scripture. Biblical associations of scholars in the United States are truly ecumenical. And committees on translations and textual criticism are composed of Catholics and Protestants. This has been so taken for granted that we tend to forget that it is a fairly recent phenomenon. And because of a common Lectionary for many of the Churches, many of us who teach Scripture regularly take part in meetings of Protestant and Catholic pastors to plan themes for the readings during Advent or Lent.

The recent pastorals of the American bishops on peace and the economy are carefully grounded in Scripture. This

100

Scripture Today

is a natural outgrowth of the emphasis on Scripture coming from Vatican II.

An important document from the Pontifical Biblical Commission on the Bible and Christology was issued in 1984. It examined eleven different scriptural approaches in Christology, and pointed out advantages and disadvantages of each approach. Finally, it emphasized both the principle of "totality," Scripture seen as a whole, as well as the particular Christologies of each New Testament author. This calls to mind the tension between the approach of Alexandria and that of Antioch. The document calls for a contemporary balance. When compared with statements of the Biblical Commission during the Modernist crisis, the tone as well as the content is completely different. The tone is positive and the content shows a remarkable expertise and balance of judgment.

Finally, the increased number of courses in Scripture in our universities shows the renewed interest in the study of Scripture in the United States. And many parish study groups also manifest this same desire of faith seeking understanding. A final assessment of Scripture today might be that it is alive and well.

IX. DISCUSSION QUESTIONS

1. Why was the witness of Scripture so important in the early Church?

2. What key texts were seen as fulfilled in the victory of the Cross and Resurrection?

3. Why did Paul seem rather indifferent to the history of Jesus "according to the flesh"?

4. In the scene of the feeding of the 5000 (Mark 6:34-44), it says that Jesus, seeing the crowd, had compassion on them, "because they were like sheep without a shepherd" (Mark 6:34). What Old Testament text(s) come(s) to mind?

5. In the same scene, what elements point to the experience of the Church?

6. In the scene of the Agony in Gethsemene (Mark

Scripture Today

14:32-42), how does the rebuke of Jesus to the sleeping disciples speak to the experience of Mark's audience?

7. Why did it take the Church so long to close the canon?

8. Why does closing the canon open it up for interpretation?

9. What are the advantages and disadvantages of the Alexandrine and the Antiochean approaches to Scripture?

10. Choose an appropriate psalm and read it from the point of view of the psalmist then, and as a prayer of Christ or the Church now. What is the difference? What is the connection?

11. With the rise of historic consciousness, how does a contemporary approach differ from that of the Middle Ages?

12. What inconsistencies do you find in the following accounts that might be signs of different sources: creation, Noah and his ark?

13. What are the problems in writing a biography of Jesus?

14. Explain some different views of Tradition and its relation to Scripture.

John L. Boyle, S. J.

15. What is your favorite Gospel and why?

16. What scene in Scripture makes you feel most involved?

17. At the death of Jesus, Matthew presents a vision of the "saints" who "had fallen asleep" being raised after the Resurrection of Jesus (Matt 27:51-54). Why is the scene placed here? What does it mean?

18. What is the difference in approach to a Gospel reading on a Sunday in Ordinary Time and during Lent or Advent?

19. In reading the parable of the Rich Man and Lazarus (Luke 16:19-31), what wider context might come to mind?

20. In a Bible study group, what are the advantages of listening to a teacher of Scripture? What are the advantages of sharing one another's reading of the text?

X. SUGGESTED READINGS

Bible Today, Collegeville: Liturgical Press.

Boadt, Lawrence. *Reading the Old Testament.* NY: Paulist, 1984.

Breck, John. *The Power of the Word.* NY: St. Vladimir's Press, 1986.

Collins, Raymond F. *Introduction to the New Testament.* NY: Image Books, 1987.

Cook, Michael L. *The Historical Jesus.* Chicago: Thomas More Press, 1986.

de Lubac, Henri. *The Sources of Revelation.* NY: Herder and Herder, 1968.

Fischer, James. *How to Read the Bible.* NY: Dodd, Mead & Co., 1987.

105

John L. Boyle, S. J.

Gabbel, John B. *The Bible as Literature.* NY: Oxford U. Press, 1986.

Gamble, H.Y. *The New Testament Canon: Its Making and Meaning.* Philadelphia: Fortress Press, 1985.

Harrington, Daniel J. *Interpreting the New Testament.* Wilmington: Michael Glazier, 1979.

Keegan, Terence J. *Interpreting the Bible.* NY: Paulist Press, 1985.

Sternberg, Meir. *The Poetics of Biblical Narrative.* Bloomington: Indiana U. Press, 1985.

Via, Dan O. Jr. *The Ethics of Mark's Gospel: In the Middle of Time.* Philadelphia: Fortress Press, 1985.